Aspects of modern sociology

The social structure of modern Britain

GENERAL EDITORS

John Barron Mays
Eleanor Rathbone Professor of Social Science, University of Liverpool

Maurice Craft
Senior Lecturer in Education, University of Exeter

Patterns of urban life

R. E. Pahl M.A., Ph.D.

Senior Lecturer in Sociology
University of Kent at Canterbury

Longmans

LONGMANS, GREEN AND CO. LTD
London and Harlow

Associated companies, branches and representatives throughout the world

© *Longmans, Green and Co. Ltd* 1970
First published 1970

SBN 582 48802 8 Cased
SBN 582 48803 6 Paper

Printed in Great Britain by
Spottiswoode, Ballantyne and Co. Ltd.,
London and Colchester

Contents

301.364
P 141

89149

Editors' preface

British higher education is now witnessing a very rapid expansion of teaching and research in the social sciences, and, in particular, in sociology. This new series has been designed for courses offered by universities, colleges of education, colleges of technology and colleges of further education to meet the needs of students training for social work, teaching and a wide variety of other professions. It does not attempt a comprehensive treatment of the whole field of sociology, but concentrates on the social structure of modern Britain which forms a central feature of most university and college sociology courses in this country. Its purpose is to offer an analysis of our contemporary society through the study of basic demographic, ideological and structural features, and through the study of such major social institutions as the family, education, the economic and political structure, and so on.

The aim has been to produce a series of introductory texts which will in combination form the basis for a sustained course of study, but each volume has been designed as a single whole and can be read in its own right.

We hope that the topics covered in the series will prove attractive to a wide reading public and that, in addition to students, others who wish to know more than is readily available about the nature and structure of their own society will find them of interest.

JOHN BARRON MAYS
MAURICE CRAFT

Foreword

Britain is physically as urbanised as any nation in the world, yet as a society we seem to be extraordinarily reluctant to accept this fact. How else can the dearth of books on urbanism and urbanisation in Britain be explained? Charles Booth and others may have pioneered the use of systematic survey techniques for documenting the urban social situation, but out of this fact-finding no systematic urban sociology has emerged. Students of the subject in this country learn more about Chicago than Glasgow or Birmingham. However, in recent years sociologically informed scholars in urban history have helped to add a new dimension to the study of urbanism in Britain. Furthermore, architects, planners and the practical professions concerned with the built environment have been pressing sociologists to systematise what is known. Thus, helped by the historians and prodded by the planners, it may be that urban sociology in Britain will enter a new phase. I hope that this book will at least show where the gaps are widest and will help to stimulate a deeper interest in the subject.

R. E. PAHL

Acknowledgements

We are indebted to the following for permission to reproduce copyright material:

Institute of Historical Research, University of London, for a table from *A History of Yorkshire: The City of York* by Edward Miller; author and The National Council of Social Service for a table from *Communities and Social Change* by Dr Mark Abrams; University of Michigan Press for a table from *The Merchant Class of Medieval London* by Sylvia L. Thrupp; author and the proprietors of *Urban Studies* for tables from *Social Class and the New Towns* by B. J. Heraud.

We also wish to thank the following for providing material from which the illustrations have been prepared: *The Economist*; Mr R. F. Greenwood; Routledge Kegan & Paul Ltd; and Mr John Westergaard of the Centre for Urban Studies for the map from the Statement of Evidence to the Royal Commission on Greater London, 1959.

The origins and growth of pre-industrial urbanism in Britain

There has been some form of urban life in Britain for nearly two thousand years. According to almost any criterion Britain is now among the most urbanised two or three nations in the world. Sociologists are interested not so much in the physical growth of towns and cities and not, even, in the proportionate increase of the population living in areas designated as urban, but rather in the changing patterns of social relationships, which may develop in urban areas. This analytical distinction between the physical situation and social relationships gives rise to certain difficulties and confusions in modern Britain, which, in many respects, may be considered to be completely urbanised in the sociological sense. These difficulties were much less apparent during the early period of the development of urban life and institutions in Britain or in western Europe generally. The town or city, even without its wall, rampart or ditch, was clearly separate and distinguishable from the country.

In this chapter I shall first consider the early colonisation and urbanisation of tribal Britain by a large bureaucratically organised and urban-based imperial power. Then, using the rather slender historical material available, I shall consider urban life and social institutions in two English preindustrial cities, York and London. This will be related to the more general sociological work of the distinguished German sociologist Max Weber, who wrote one of the pioneer works in urban sociology early in this century. More recently the American sociologist Gideon Sjoberg has written on preindustrial cities and we shall also consider his contribution. It should be stressed that I am not so much concerned with telling a story, inferring that what comes before is directly related to what follows; rather

I am concerned with specifically sociological themes, which may be discussed in the light of the available historical evidence. The main focus is on social institutions and social relationships.

THE BEGINNINGS OF URBAN SOCIETY AND URBAN IDEOLOGIES

Tribal Britain was administered from fortified camps which some people have described as towns. However, it was the conquest and colonisation by the Roman legionaries and administrators that introduced cities to Britain. In many ways the Roman Empire was the creation of the city and Roman intellectuals had much the same ambivalent attitudes towards urbanism as contemporary intellectuals (Lowenstein, 1965).

Many authors in ancient Rome complained of the noise, the traffic and the crowds. Horace complained of 'that bit of Hell/Known as big city life', and Martial complained of the transience or superficiality of certain urban social relationships—'in all the city there is no man who is so near and yet so far from me' as his own nextdoor neighbour. The jaded satirists not only deplored the physical form and pattern of urban life but also the source of income of the rich; Horace wrote:

> Some men derive their income from government contracts;
> Some hunt down rich widows, with fruit and glazed candy;
> Some cast their nets for old men to put in their fishponds;
> Some people's capital keeps on growing, kept growing
> By interest (fostered by time, just like a tree).

In the sophisticated city, life was claimed to be vile and corrupt whereas the good life could be lived in the country: after all, as Varro put it—'God made the country and man made the town'. Typically, the rich got the best of both worlds: 'Whenever worn out with worry, I wish to sleep, I go to my villa', remarked Martial, and Pliny was obliged to commute to peace at his villa 'but seventeen miles distant from Rome; so that having finished your affairs in town,

you can spend the night here after completing a full working day.'
Yet there were, of course, dissenting voices; Cicero did not enjoy
life in the country: 'I cannot describe how ardently I long for town,
how hard I find it to bear the stupidity of life here.' Even Horace
makes one of his characters in his *Satires* laugh at him:

'At Rome, you yearn
For the country, but once in the sticks, you praise to high heaven
The far off city, you nitwit.'

Although urban life was the basis of the ancient Mediterranean
civilisations it was not easy to establish it in tribal parts of the Empire
like Britain. The Romans adopted a policy of creating what French
geographers have described in once French-occupied Africa as bino-
cular towns—the Roman town was built adjoining the tribal camp.
This system had the advantage of close proximity to the old tribal
aristocracy who were responsible for levying local taxes; the unit of
administration was based on the existing tribal area and the urban
network became the main source of British Romanisation. However,
most Roman towns were simply military camps and only five British
towns had a status which enabled their inhabitants to have the
rights of Roman citizenship. One of these, Verulamium (St Albans),
may have been a *municipium*, which would have merited its own
charter and constitution, but this is still in dispute. Archaeological
evidence has shown that Verulamium certainly had pretensions to
grandeur. At the peak of its prosperity there were large triumphal
arches, temples, an openair theatre and a forum with large centrally
heated houses built in a prosperous colonial style in brick and tile. In
his report on the recent excavations at Verulamium S. S. Frere suggested that the more wealthy men of the Catuvellauni tribe invested
their money in blocks of shops fronting Watling Street.

Acculturation followed urban development: Tacitus describes
how Agricola provided educational facilities for the sons of tribal
chiefs so that 'in place of distaste for the Latin language came a
passion to command it. In the same way, our national dress came into
favour and the toga was everywhere to be seen. And so the Britons
were gradually led on to the amenities that make vice agreeable—

3

arcades, baths and sumptuous banquets. They spoke of such novelties as "civilisation", when really they were only a feature of enslavement' (Tacitus, p. 72).

It is difficult to believe that this period of some three hundred years of urbanisation and Romanisation did not have some lasting effects. Substantial villas were built in the countryside by the new gentry, with masonry footings, mosaic floors, bath-houses, heated rooms, and glazed windows. Even if towns declined between the Saxon invasions and the Norman conquest a more sophisticated urban style may have continued amongst a scattered Romano-British population, which could have provided the basis for the merchant-trader class which appeared in the eighth and ninth centuries. And the withdrawal of the Roman legions in the fifth century may not have led to quite the eclipse of urban life that some historians have claimed. As Professor Edward Miller (1961) put it: 'There seems, in fact, every reason to believe that seventh-century townsmen were fully conscious of the origins of the Roman monuments around them. In York the massive walls and columns of the earlier culture . . . must have inspired even farmer and artisan with some sense of urban community.' York maintained a strong urban tradition from the fifth to the tenth centuries. Canterbury also maintained its urban tradition and as early as the ninth century there is reference to a Cnihtengild—an organisation for a defined section of the town, although who the Cnihts of Canterbury were is not clear. These early urban voluntary associations are forerunners of the medieval guilds. Regulations for a thegns' guild at Cambridge are mainly concerned with the rituals connected with the blood feud but there is also some concern with funeral dues, the transport of a member's body home if he is taken ill or dies outside the district, and so on.

It is likely that in some English urban centres trade and industry carried on through the Dark Ages. Nevertheless there is dispute among historians whether, apart from London and one or two other places, there were any real towns in Anglo-Saxon England. Certainly many burghs were closely integrated into the rural economy with little that could be described as distinctly urban in any sociological sense. However, evidence is accumulating of quite considerable urban development. For example, in the ninth and tenth centuries the Anglo-Danish town of Thetford developed a broad industrial and trading structure. Metalsmiths worked iron and copper and there was a flourishing woollen and pottery industry. Trade extended all over eastern England and to the Continent. Other inhabitants of the town were farmers providing the food for the industrial workers. The site of the town extended for about a mile along the Little Ouse valley and stretched inland for half a mile. At the time of the Domesday Survey in 1086 Thetford was an administrative and commercial centre comparable with Norwich or Oxford and had maybe 4,000 or 5,000 inhabitants. York probably had more than 8,000 inhabitants and was divided into smaller units known as 'shires'. London probably had 12,000 inhabitants, though Domesday evidence is lacking. At the end of the eleventh century perhaps a tenth of England's population lived permanently in towns and even if many of these towns' inhabitants were farmers there was a substantial minority of urban Englishmen, legally and politically distinct and apart from the manorial structure.

However, the early urbanisation of Britain by the Romans and merchants is obscure, largely owing to the lack of documentary evidence. It is nonetheless possible that if a tenth of the population did live permanently in towns by the end of the eleventh century then England was more urbanised than Africa is today. Of course this statement is difficult to substantiate, since much depends on the definition of 'town', the occupational structure of the urban population, and so on.

PREINDUSTRIAL URBANISM

Max Weber has argued that the only time and place where the true urban community has existed was in medieval Europe. Such a community, he asserted, should be based primarily on trade and commerce and generally had the following features:

1. Fortification
2. A market

3. A court of its own and at least partially autonomous law
4. A related form of association
5. At least partial autonomy with burghers taking part in the election of urban administrators.

Essentially, then, the city emerges out of feudal society as a distinct and largely autonomous community. 'City air makes one free' was an adage in medieval Germany and in England a serf who escaped to town and lived unchallenged within its walls for a year and a day could claim to be regarded as a free man. Generally, urban dwellers belonged to professional groups such as crafts or guilds, localised within the urban areas. Within the ward or street districts urbanites had specific responsibilities for maintaining the peace: social control was maintained both formally and informally.

Weber suggested that such ideas of 'urban citizenry' or 'urban community' appear to be lacking in Far Eastern cities. Cities acting specifically as cities, as a particular kind of communal action, are the product of a distinctively European tradition. Urban freehold, property and trade were the bases of the class of burghers, independent of the feudal lords. 'During the period of maximum autonomy', Weber remarks, 'the cities displayed an exceptional variety of forms and trends.' Some cities pursued imperialistic foreign policies, having their own soldiers and even controlling overseas colonies. Some large cities in Italy and Germany achieved an international political importance. This was not the pattern in England where cities were always limited in their power, largely because, although the king did grant charters allowing a degree of autonomy to cities from the twelfth century, crucial military and political power was centralised in a way which made English feudalism quite a separate sort of system from that which developed in France or Germany.

Perhaps the best way to see preindustrial cities is by analysing the sources and distribution of power. Firstly, there was the power struggle between the individual cities and the central authority. Secondly, there was a struggle between cities for various privileges and trade monopolies, particularly the struggle between the overwhelmingly dominant London and other cities. And, finally, there were struggles within the city for political power, trade and craft privilege, the rights of minorities and so on. The city as a sociological fact could not exist without its power.

Professor Sjoberg has described other characteristics, which, he claims, are typically found in an ideal type of preindustrial city. In terms of spatial arrangements he mentions the segregation of minority ethnic groups, the congestion within the walls, the dominance of the central area and low functional differentiation. He sees a direct link between the technological base of a society and the localisation of particular crafts and merchant activities in segregated quarters or streets. Such preindustrial cities are essentially centres for the elite: only there can they communicate and maintain their common interests. 'The more potent the elite the grander the city.' The elite has power rationalised through religion and maintained through the control of education and government. Sjoberg argues that the merchants are excluded from the elite, despite the city being dependent on commerce. 'Business men, or merchants, fall into the lower class or outcaste group.' The social structure is said to be rigid and there is very little social mobility. The economic structure is based on the guilds. Most economic transactions are concluded after long haggling. There is little specialisation of function in craft industrial production, although there is a good deal of product specialisation.

Sjoberg also discusses marriage and the family, the political structure, the religious structure and so on. His book has given rise to a great deal of controversy and he has been severely criticised by historians and sociologists, largely for generalising about *the* preindustrial city which, he claims, has common characteristics remaining much the same 'over fifty-five centuries' and between different cultures. Such broad generalisations are sharply at variance with the work of Weber, who stressed the variation and distinctiveness of preindustrial cities largely as reflections of the distribution of power in society. There may, indeed, be certain similarities between contemporary 'preindustrial' cities in Africa or Asia and medieval European 'preindustrial' cities, but to argue that they are essentially the same type in that they are all 'preindustrial' is hardly defensible.

7

Not only does Sjoberg, in Wrigley's phrase, do violence to history (Wrigley, 1967, p. 53), but he also does violence to sociology. Nevertheless his work is widely read and quoted.

It is in this context that the following, more detailed, accounts of York and London should be seen. We are still a very long way from a sociological theory of preindustrial urbanism and urbanisation in Britain. Quite apart from the intrinsic interest of such a study, it is important to understand that cities are not simply products of the last two hundred years. The industrial revolution may have helped to form an urban society but the distinctiveness of urban life was, in certain respects, more marked in the centuries which preceded it.

MEDIEVAL YORK: THE EMERGENCE OF URBAN AUTONOMY

Medieval York provides an example of the working of the distinctive urban institutions of a community of traders and craftsmen (Miller, 1961). Until the year 1212 the sheriff of Yorkshire had to provide revenues for the king and these were probably derived from tolls and other charges on the trading activities of the citizens, a simple tax on domestic property and revenue from the urban court. Furthermore, the king imposed extra levies: between 1156 and 1206 there were sixteen of these, yielding some £3,500, which would be a considerable burden on the citizens. In the later part of the twelfth century the citizens were granted the right to found an association to manage the internal trade of the city, linking up with associations on the coast and in Normandy. Nevertheless, it is interesting that some basic civic liberties are thought to have been laid down without the warrant of a charter so that even as early as the beginning of the twelfth century such rights of citizenship may have been established for some time.

In the early years of the thirteenth century the citizens of York were given the collective responsibility for the management of urban finances, thus emancipating them from the power of the sheriff. Later in the same century citizens acquired further legal rights—for example, they could be convicted only by a jury of fellow citizens, except when the city as a whole was charged. Legal, financial and commercial autonomy meant that the citizens had effectively preempted the authority of the sheriff and were, by the mid-thirteenth century, directly responsible to the central government. Even so, it is important to emphasise that, unlike some continental cities, York was not truly independent: all her privileges were dependent upon the king's grace.

During the thirteenth century York gradually acquired its distinct civic constitution. It had a mayor from about 1212 and other officers such as coroners, chamberlains (or financial officers) and a beadle were appointed soon afterwards. Citizens were expected to play an active part in self government: the butchers' guild was responsible for the city gaol at night and parishes had formal responsibilities connected with the apprehension of escaped prisoners. A small ruling elite provided the mayors during this period and it was common for the same man to be re-elected five or six times and then for his son to follow afterwards. A recurring problem during the century was the inability of the citizens to raise sufficient revenue to meet the demands of the national Exchequer: this may have been due partly to the fact that 'prominent citizens' had certain tax privileges which were not available to the 'lesser folk'. This was a source of social tension which in some towns produced serious urban riots. The urban elite of thirteenth-century York appeared to have little sense of *noblesse oblige*: as the city's historian Edward Miller puts it: 'The civic officers failed to act on royal writs, took bribes, levied excessive charges on bakers, and hanged out of hand a man accused of theft when he made certain accusations against some of the *majores* of the city.'

An extremely important right held by the citizens of York was the ability to own, inherit and sell private property. Urban tenements are likely to have changed hands frequently and a body of tenurial custom emerged constituting a *lex civitatis* different in many important respects from the common law of England. The evolution of urban customs into what were in effect civic by-laws was an important element in the development of a distinctive urban consciousness.

A further source of tension in the urban situation developed between the ecclesiastical elite, concerned to defend its distinctive rights and privileges, and the lay urban government. The mayor and

citizens were disinclined to respect exemptions from various tolls
and taxes at a time of financial difficulties. Running battles between
the ecclesiastical and civic elites continued through the century.

Social and geographic mobility and rural-urban linkages

The growth of York was based on a high level of immigration, which
continued to the end of the Middle Ages. Migrants from the surrounding villages added to the Anglo-Scandinavian core of the city
and helped to counterbalance the high urban mortality. A wide range
of places throughout northern England provided the source of these
migrants who maintained links with their rural kinship networks.
Cities provided a crucial avenue of social mobility from the constraints of rural feudal society but it was probably necessary for
those with few resources to have a patron who could help to ease the
transition to urban-based networks and urban institutions.

It is extremely difficult to say anything precise about the social
processes in a medieval city. There are, however, lists of the men
admitted to the freedom of the city. During Edward I's reign, for
example,

TABLE I

City of York: admissions to freedom 1272–1509

Craft groups	Per cent of known occupations				
	1272–1306	1307–1349	1350–1399	1400–1449	1450–1509
Textile	7	14	28	21	21
Provision	29	23	11	14	17
Mercantile	10	16	16	15	11
Leather	30	22	15	12	13
Building	2	3	6	8	7
Metal	17	13	11	11	10
Miscellaneous	5	9	13	19	21
% freemen whose occupation is not stated	40	23	12	11	9
Total freemen	767	2540	4838	4870	4086
Av. freemen/yr	26	59	97	97	68

Source: Miller, 1961.

it seems that some 30 per cent of these were craftsmen in the leather trade and those engaged in the provision trades comprised 29 per cent. The remaining freemen fell into the following categories: metal crafts 17 per cent; commerce and shipping 10 per cent; textile crafts, mainly tailors 7 per cent; miscellaneous occupations 5 per cent; and building crafts, 2 per cent. It does appear that this community of craftsmen, working for a restricted market, had within it broad extremes of wealth. In a tax return of 1204, out of a total of £375, thirty-two men contributed £212 between them: of these ten paid £10 or more, four from £5–£10, three from £1–£5 and fifteen under £1. Men with considerable wealth appear to be very few indeed: these were the merchants who provided the city's elite. Some of these merchants acquired extensive property—both in the city and in the rural areas; some provided loans to country landowners. All this helped to ensure permanent links between urban and rural areas and helps to explain the stability of York's ruling elite in the twelfth and thirteenth centuries.

The emergence of a community power structure

We are told that 'it was a tight little group which ruled the city at this time' and we can be more sure of this since it is the wills and other records of the very rich people that remain for the historian to correlate. The records of the poor are scant. The city's liberties continued to be extended in the fourteenth century but the power of the ruling elite remained concentrated—in the half-century ending in 1372 only fifteen names appear in the list of mayors. By the end of the century candidates for the mayoral election were restricted to aldermen. Royal intervention in the later fifteenth century attempted to let the crafts have greater power in the election of aldermen. This threat to the oligarchical power of the mayoralty was resisted: yet the property owners' power could not be maintained. Out of eighty-eight mayors between 1399 and 1509 one was a glazier, one a spicer, one a pewterer, and one a vintner; there were three drapers, four grocers and goldsmiths, and five dyers; but sixty-eight were merchants or mercers. To quote Professor Miller again: 'So far as the mayorality is a measure of it, the government of late medieval York was not so much an aldermanic as a mercantile oligarchy. It was the merchant who had stepped into the place of the property-owning patrician of earlier times.' Furthermore

A small, close knit oligarchy filled civic offices and seats in the council chamber. More than that, these men were bound by ties of occupation. As early as 1378–9 the aldermen appear to have been drawn exclusively, and the councillors preponderantly, from the class of wealthy traders. Of the 1420 council, five belonged to manufacturing crafts, but two were drapers and twenty-two merchants. York was ruled not merely by an oligarchy, but by a mercantile oligarchy.

This does little to support Sjoberg's notion of the relationship between the merchant and the elite mentioned above.

Craft organisation

It is difficult to know how many guilds there were in York: various lists give between fifty and eighty names of crafts but industrial activities were very finely graded and there was a good deal of trespassing on others' province. There were also various amalgamations and combinations. The ordinances of the guilds were drawn up by the masters of the craft but received their force from enforcement by the city authorities, and hence guild officers were responsible to both the city council and their craft. This responsibility for industrial organisation on the part of the city meant that civic authorities arbitrated in disputes between guilds—indeed the city had the power to disband guilds if they were completely recalcitrant.

The most important guild officer was the searcher, who was appointed by his predecessor and was answerable to the city authorities for the standards of workmanship in their craft. Searchers summoned guild meetings, managed its finances, 'searched' the articles made by guild members, approved the technical skill of new masters and of 'strangers' coming to the city, authorised the taking on of apprentices, and often inspected the quality of 'foreign' goods coming into the city. The carpenters employed four searchers and also an employment officer for their craft. Often other men were appointed to help the searchers assess penalties. Other guild regulations included the prohibition of night work, work done outside a master's house, and the employment of more than one apprentice by a master. Officers of the guild controlled entry, ensured that 'foreigns' had appropriate testimonials and took the entrance fee of 20s. All these rules supported jointly by city and guild were to maintain quality control in the interests of local consumer or export merchant.

Apprentices normally had to serve for seven years and the industrial unit was generally limited to the master, his wife and one apprentice, perhaps supplemented by journeymen or servants. In 1401 the searchers of the spurriers' guild allotted immigrant labour to the master whose need was greatest due to lack, death, or illness of a servant. Later in the century immigrant workers had attempted to organise collective action to negotiate better wage rates. 'The city authorities intervened and forbade servants to form their own organisations or to persuade other servants to leave their master or the city. On the other hand a master was to pay a workman for whom temporarily he had no employment, and piece rates were amended generally in an upward direction.' By no means all apprentices became freemen: 'In 1482-3, out of sixty-five apprentices who completed their terms, only thirty-eight became freemen forthwith. The rest paid a lower fee to pursue their callings in the city, presumably as journeymen, though some of them became freemen in later years.' Yet the activities of guilds were not limited to economic affairs: they also operated as charities, giving alms and associating themselves with religious activities, particularly the famous Corpus Christi plays.

The urban social structure

Inequalities of wealth in medieval York have already been mentioned: a further tax return of 1327 shows that only one man had goods worth more than £26 and only fifty-five (7 per cent) at £5 or more. On the other hand 61 per cent were assessed at between £1 and £4 and 32 per cent had goods worth less than £1. Clearly very few men were wealthy and of these only a fifth were merchants, the rest being craftsmen of various sorts. Whilst there was clearly a hard core of urban poor the poll tax returns of 1377 show that a third of all taxpayers had servants. However, whereas only a few craftsmen had a servant, merchants generally had five or six and one had eight.

THE SOCIAL SIGNIFICANCE OF THE METROPOLIS

The social composition of medieval London

In medieval England London was a unique city in size and organisation, resembling more the great continental cities rather than the larger provincial centres, such as York or Bristol, compared with which it was at least three times as large. In 1501–2 Thrupp has calculated that there were some 3,400 citizens out of a population of some 30 or 40 thousand. Only those who had sworn loyalty to the city government and had undertaken to bear their share of taxation and public duty could style themselves as citizens or free men and claim the various privileges that were guaranteed to the community by royal charter. Those who were unenfranchised were 'outsiders' whether born in or outside London and were termed 'foreigns': these were often the poor—the porters, water carriers and casual labourers, some of whom came in from the suburbs and surrounding country. In 1463 the city authorities attempted to keep foreign shopkeepers segregated. Those who were born overseas were called 'aliens'.

TABLE 2
London population 1501–2

Citizens			Estimates of total persons
Merchants	1,200	with wives, children and apprentices	6,300
Other citizens in company livery	1,200	with wives, children and apprentices	6–7,000
		aliens of superior rank	500
Small masters and workers	2,000	with wives, single women, children and apprentices	7,000
		foreigns, small masters and workers with families including suburban population	10,000
		aliens, small masters and workers with families including suburban population	2,500

Source: Thrupp, 1948, p. 51.

Social and geographical mobility and rural-urban linkages

London's links with the rest of the country were wide ranging: from perhaps the twelfth, and certainly the thirteenth century onwards, citizens were buying country property, not simply as an investment but also as a pleasant place to live. The subsidy roll of 1436 shows that citizens' country properties were scattered in almost every English county except the far north. These properties satisfied the merchant's love of business, pleasure, and display but the country was also considered a healthier place to be, particularly in times of urban epidemics. 'I undyrstonde they dy sor in London', wrote one merchant urging his brother to come out to his place in Essex. Building new manor houses in the country was as popular as the improvement and renovation of existing property in need of attention. Apparently many of the merchants and other rich men of London had been brought up in the country either being entrusted as babies to village nurses or spending long holidays in the country. These childhood memories may have helped to retain an affection for rural life amongst the merchant class, many of whom set themselves up in country houses near London. Even when elected mayor at the end of the fifteenth century, John Warde tried to continue living in Hertfordshire and only the threat of a £500 fine brought him and his family into town. Retirement into the country was popular—mainly in the home counties.

Both merchants and members of lesser companies must have maintained kinship links with provincial towns and rural areas: evidence from London wills shows that they were anxious to leave generous legacies to country kin. Sometimes executors were instructed to distribute money among poor relations or to the poor of the neighbourhood in their 'country'.

Movement from the merchant class into the landed gentry was often achieved by buying a country property: older families might consider the merchant who maintained his London connections as simply a *nouveau riche*, but if he had been a sheriff, alderman or, better still, mayor then he could certainly gain status. Marrying his daughter into the local gentry was one of the surest ways of a family acquiring superior status in the second generation.

Not only did the merchants take London into the provinces, London also drew on the rest of the country and indeed, without a steady stream of immigration, the population would have dwindled. The merchant class could not have maintained itself without recruitment from outside and this would apply with even more force to the other citizens and the unenfranchised. From early in the fourteenth century, therefore, London was recruiting apprentices from the whole country. Thrupp shows that the main area of recruitment shifted from the home counties through the Midlands to the north as the century progressed. Some indication of this is shown by an analysis of the wills of rich merchants who left money to people in the area in which they were born.

TABLE 3
Wills of rich merchants

Region of birth	Merchants dying 1450–1515 (N=139)
	%
Home Counties	24
East	27
Midlands	28
North	10
West	9

Source: Thrupp, 1948, p. 210.

Thrupp suggests that apprentices were recruited from diverse social origins and many merchants came from the trading and artisan elements in the villages and small towns. Others had been trained in larger towns and were able to buy themselves the freedom of the city. At the end of the fifteenth century perhaps between a third and a half of all immigrant apprentices, who were being accepted in the main London companies, came from families already engaged in industry and trade, mostly in the smaller towns and villages.

The social and demographic impact of London on the provinces in the sixteenth and seventeenth centuries.

London as a capital city grew to be the largest city in Europe by the end of the seventeenth century. Quite apart from its importance as the home of the Royal Court and the Courts of Justice it was also a centre of conspicuous consumption for the nation's gentry. With its many private schools and the Inns of Court it developed so rapidly as an educational centre that the historian F. J. Fisher estimated that by the reign of Charles I 'the majority of the country's gentry' were spending the most impressionable years of their lives there. And even when they were settled on their estate London was still of outstanding importance as a centre of litigation, as a money market, as the centre of the political world and, of course, as the source of a bride with a large dowry (Fisher, 1943).

As it became the custom of the gentry to winter in London, luxury trades expanded and King James complained of 'Those swarms of gentry who, through the instigation of their wives and to new-model and fashion their daughters (who if they were unmarried marred their reputations, and if married lost them) did neglect their country hospitality, and cumber the city, a general nuisance to the kingdom' (quoted in Fisher, 1948). So much for swinging London!

Given the rapid population growth of London—that is the addition of some 275,000 between 1650 and 1750—then an average of 8,000 immigrants a year over the period would be needed to cover the shortfall of births over deaths. In a recent paper E. A. Wrigley (1967) has made some very interesting calculations. He assumes that since it is the young and unmarried who are most likely to migrate and since this category would represent a birth population half as large again and since, finally, the average surplus of births over deaths in provincial England was 5 per thousand per annum, then London's growth was absorbing the natural increase of a population of some $2\frac{1}{2}$ million! This is even more remarkable when one remembers that the population of England, excluding London, was only about 5 million at this time and that in many areas of the West and North there was little natural increase or indeed there was a decrease in these areas.

In the light of these calculations and assumptions Wrigley claims that one-sixth, or an even higher fraction, of the total adult population of England 'at some stage of their lives had direct experience of life in the great city'.

This raises many interesting and important questions: what were the qualitative differences, if any, between London and the provinces? If urbanisation as concentration had given way to urbanisation as a form of cultural diffusion in the hundred years before the conventional beginning of the industrial revolution, what does this tell us about the nature of English urbanism? Maybe the important distinction is not between town and country but between London and the provinces. Local landed society could dominate a provincial town in a way which would not be possible in London.

The emergence of industrial urbanism in Britain

In 1801, 9·73 per cent of the population of England and Wales lived in London and only a further 7·21 per cent lived in towns of 20,000 people or more. But by the middle of the century the urban population of Britain was greater than the rural, and indeed, since 1911 four-fifths of the population have lived in areas defined as urban. The period from the 1840s to the 1870s showed the most rapid rates of urbanisation, although places such as Manchester, which doubled its size in the first thirty years of the nineteenth century were ahead of the national pattern. The growth and establishing of the northern towns was largely due to high rates of natural increase of the population in the rural areas and country towns immediately surrounding the booming industrial centres. There is very little evidence to suggest that there was anything in the way of a drift to the industrial north from the rural south.

The detailed pattern of population growth and mobility in the nineteenth century still remains to be described and analysed. Some counties show a rapid growth of population, due to natural increase, whereas others do not. Much depended on local employment conditions for men, women, and children. Some skilled workers may have been considerably mobile, moving about the country with their families from one job to another in a series of relatively short moves. On the other hand less skilled workers may have been much less mobile. The important point is that the aggregate figures of urban growth and population movement in the nineteenth century give a very oversimplified view and may be positively misleading if one is concerned with what happened in particular regions or localities.

Places such as Middlesborough or Barrow-in-Furness grew up as boom towns almost overnight. In 1864 Barrow had a population of 8,176, a trebling of the population in three years. Such breakneck urbanisation meant that houses were thrown up quickly and cheaply; local government barely existed, if at all, and in many places there was no provision for any services. An article in *The Times* of 8 February 1871 on the problems of administering the census, illustrates the situation very graphically:

There are many towns containing long lines of cottaged streets, formed by the gradual coalescence of buildings erected by several small proprietors; and in such streets it's not uncommon for each proprietor to give his little road a distinctive name, and to number the houses it contains from one upwards, without the smallest regard to the numbers in the vicinity. In Nottingham there was formerly a long street which was said to repeat its numbers up to three no less than 30 times. . . . A resident there would give his address as 'The fifth number 3 on the right hand side as you go up', for such names as 'Matilda Place' or 'Eliza Cottages' had long been swept away.

These boom towns of course had to rely heavily on migration, often from Scotland or Ireland, and 'little Irelands' appeared in many northern industrial towns. Nevertheless, the more general pattern was for migrants to travel short distances.

COLONISATION AND THE INDUSTRIAL VILLAGE

Industrialisation did not necessarily imply urbanisation. Many industrialists preferred to have their workpeople close to the works, not only to ensure punctuality but also as a means of social control. T. Chalmers was urging in the 1820s in a three volume work on *The Christian and Civic Economy of Large Towns* that cities should be split into smaller localities in order to prevent the people 'forming into a combined array of hostile feeling and prejudice'. Industrialists were alert to the dangers of 'the unmanageable mass' and saw many advantages of an employment monopoly in an industrial village. Many industrial villages in Lancashire remained self-sufficient, independent communities and such villages also existed within borough boundaries. These 'urban' villages may well have had as strong a sense of separateness as those industrial villages in more rural setting. Where the employer played the benevolent-squire role, contributing to schools, bathhouses and the Mechanics Institute, then, as the urban historian J. D. Marshall puts it, 'the idiocy of village life might be rejuvenated and even strengthened in its industrial context' (Marshall, 1968, p. 226). Of course, whether this is sociologically accurate is largely a matter of conjecture.

This planting of new communities, or colonisation, whether adjacent to existing centres or out in the country—the primary colonisation—was a common situation in north-west England. Urbanisation in the nineteenth century is generally thought of as being a matter of huge concentrations of population. This parallel development of industrial decentralisation must not be overlooked. It created a distinctive form of urbanism. For example, Barrow's social development centred on a series of colonies, in turn dependent on a succession of industries stimulated into being by the initial act of investment; an iron-working colony populated by Staffordshire migrants, a group of ore-mining communities on the periphery, one at least consisting almost entirely of Cornwall miners, and soon afterwards, a shipbuilding community containing a strong Clydebank element and housed, appropriately, in Glasgow-type tenements.

This multicellular structure had important sociological implications, such as the growth of separate formal associations for each cell or community. The statistics describing urban growth in the nineteenth century may imply a stronger rural-urban dichotomy than was in fact the case. Sociologists, such as the American Louis Wirth, who argue that the size, population density and social heterogeneity of urban areas necessarily have qualitative effects on patterns of behaviour, and social relationships have misled us into assuming that a limited number of quantitative indices can be associated with precise social effects. Urbanisation is a very good example of this. Describing the mere size of different places at different periods of time may have very little sociological significance. For example, the great tin-plate industry of Swansea led to a flood of immigration to the area throughout the nineteenth century, but Swansea as a town in a sociological sense has never existed. Rosser and Harris (1965, p. 66) remark: 'Individual families do not live *in* Swansea but rather one of the many neighbourhoods or communities *within* Swansea. . . . The important and effective sociological unit is the local community rather than the Borough as a whole.' Places such as Bury and Blackburn were also made up of colonies of speculative housing surrounding the scattered factories of individual owners. It would then be wrong to assume that all the new and expanding towns of the British industrial revolution followed the model of grid-iron expansion from the centre outwards, which may have been the typical American pattern.

URBANISM AND CLASS-CONSCIOUSNESS IN NINETEENTH-CENTURY TOWNS

Historical urban sociology hardly exists in this country and so we have had to make do with Engels's description of the working class in Manchester or Booth's description of London at the end of the nineteenth century and the work of non-sociologically informed historians. Hence we know very little indeed about the process of urbanisation, seen not merely as an aggregation of population within certain administrative areas, but rather, qualitatively, as the restructuring of social relationships within an urban-industrial milieu. The most dramatic sociological consequence of the various technological and other changes, which we term the industrial revolution, was the crystallisation of a class society.

Economic and social historians have debated amongst themselves how much *real* poverty there was in nineteenth century towns, how bad the health and housing may have been and other such problems, mostly defined by the Reports and Royal Commissions of contemporary social reformers. The dramatic emergence of an urban-industrial society created new social conditions as well as new physical conditions. How did these newly created and expanding towns react as social entities? There has been a welcome development of an interest among historians in community history and local social systems at previous periods of time; but just as no modern industrial sociologist would expect to find the same response under different technological systems and work situations, so also should the urban sociologist expect different urban systems to invoke different responses.

Recent research by John Foster, a Cambridge historian, provides an example of the kind of urban history of most interest to urban sociologists. He undertook careful historical analysis of what he terms 'the class dimension' in Oldham, Northampton, and South Shields in the early nineteenth century. He was concerned with the immediate context that moulded a man's social behaviour: whom he married, where he lived, how he worked and what he hoped for. In a phrase, he was looking at the differential life chances in different industrial-urban situations. Foster analysed the various social categories of his town in terms of occupation, industry, birthplace, family structure and so on, and also analysed marriage certificates in order to assess how open or closed specific status groups were. Finally, he analysed the available documentary evidence in order to test his hypotheses about class-consciousness in particular. The results are some extremely penetrating case studies of the class reactions to emerging industrial-urbanism. What follows is a direct paraphrase of his work.

Oldham

In Oldham by 1851 two-thirds of the borough's labour force of 40,000 were employed in the coal-mining, cotton and engineering industries. These industries were highly capitalised, with control concentrated with a small number of families; for example, 80 per cent of the engineering workers were employed by three big firms. There was very little chance of social mobility and there had not been much chance during the early period of capitalisation: all except one of the early cotton firms were founded by small landowners switching over from out-work manufacturing. These yeomen manufacturers had been building up their capital from the mid-eighteenth century.

Thus at mid-century there were 12,000 worker families selling their labour to seventy capitalist families. The capitalist families were very rich—annual incomes ranged between £3,000 and £10,000—and most owned estates in other parts of the country. Incomes of worker *families* ranged from £50 to £100—insufficient to keep any but the top 15 per cent of highly-paid craft workers *permanently* out of primary poverty. One worker child in five died before its first birthday. One female mill worker in every seven died while in the age group 25–34 (mostly of TB). One miner in every five could expect to be killed during a normal working life. Up to 1850 mill hours were never much below 12 a day, six days a week. Nor could the system guarantee even this minimal existence. There were the regular periods of mass unemployment—sending the proportion of families in primary poverty at *any one time* well over 40 per cent. This was the class situation with which people had to come to terms. For the first 50 years of the century their reaction was to fight it (Foster, 1968, pp. 284–5).

For a period of fifty years from the 1790s through to the 1840s a small group of people worked consistently to overthrow the system. By controlling the police for a period, together with certain other local powers, the working class maintained a measure of control. They were able to do this by threatening to boycott local shopkeepers unless they voted appropriately at local elections. The essential precondition of class formation, argues Foster, following Marx, is that people *think* it is possible to change things. He brings forward a number of contemporary statements and accounts which support his contention that the workers were analysing the local situation in terms of class. For example, the following is part of a resolution passed in 1838 at a mass meeting of Oldham workers:

. . . that labour is the source of all property; without a surplus of labour has been performed and property produced no accumulation of property can take place . . . that it is an indisputable fact that the various classes of capitalists have the whole power of making and administering the laws, which is almost uniformly done for their own benefit . . . that the time has now come when Englishmen must learn to act instead of talk (quoted in Foster, 1968, p. 289).

Foster argues that this degree of working-class solidarity required considerable organisation and mobilisation, both to keep control of local government and to prevent class splitting up into status groups as a means of accommodating social inequality. Partly there was simply coercion by the workers of the workers to maintain this solidarity. However, Foster also produces evidence to show that marriages between labourers and highly paid craftsmen were far more frequent than in South Shields, where there was no class conflict and where there was a highly developed hierarchy of occupational neighbourhoods. For more than a generation the social structure in Oldham, below the seventy capitalist families, remained remarkably open.

The local bourgeoisie was similarly remarkably united. Foster was able to analyse friendship clusterings, that is to say groups of people who went to each other's weddings and funerals and acted as mutual executors. Those with substantial capital were closely tied together by kinship and marriage into a closeknit network. Within this network were two main clusterings. The 'traditional' bourgeoisie lived in quasirural situations on land they had occupied for centuries, growing richer as the men who worked for them grew poorer. The other cluster Foster terms 'cosmopolitan', many of these also had traditional peasant backgrounds but now employed labour in the crowded central core of the town. They did not develop social relationships locally as much as with others in Manchester and the County aristocracy.

Between the capitalists and the workers was a very small 'middle class' of tradesmen, small employers and masters. Such a group had a limited stake in the system and shared a common belief that they were hard done by. The small man, despised and intimidated, fighting grimly for economic survival, watched the town's bourgeoisie taking its annual 10 per cent while their own neighbours appeared one by one in the bankruptcy court. The tradesmen (town centre food wholesalers, drapers, printers, corn millers, etc.) were mainly concerned with keeping their working capital intact (rarely above £5,000) and maintaining their essential links with outside supplies and customers. The greatest recurrent threat to a family's working capital (and its trading connections) was a series of bad marriages. The group therefore kept exclusively together, insulating its members from undesirable contacts. The little masters (commission spinners, waste dealers, millwright, jobbing builders and so on) had little use for working capital or outside links. They worked for local markets and needed only skill in their trade and an ability to organise small-scale production. They tended to merge socially if not politically with the working class.

This, then, is the class society in Oldham in the early nineteenth century as analysed by Foster. How does this compare with other nineteenth century towns with different patterns of industrial-urbanism?

Northampton

At the beginning of the nineteenth century Northampton mainly served as a supply centre for the county's landed society or as an agricultural market. In the 1820s and 1830s people moved in to the developing shoe industry from the surrounding countryside so that by 1851, with a population of 26,000, almost half the labour force was employed in the shoe industry. Production, requiring no fixed capital, was organised on garret sweat-shop lines, and London merchants mostly supplied the credit and made the profits. Northampton had none of the tight completeness of Oldham in its community structure. Tory hoteliers and lawyers, Whig-dissenter corn and wool dealers and radical garret masters split elite politics in three ways. Even though primary poverty was, if anything, more severe than in Oldham, nevertheless class formation was slight. 'Working-class' politics remained those of an occupational subgroup—not of labour as a whole. The old hierarchical status system held up. The workers moved from the village to the town but the old county aristocracy were not far away. The shopmen, coachwrights, furniture makers, and brewery workers remained Anglican and deferential. For the shoemakers the unemployment and poverty in the countryside, which they had just left, contrasted unfavourably with their immediate situation and perhaps distracted attention from it.

South Shields

The situation in Shields was different again. Half the labour force was organised round shifting coal down to London. There were 200 ships distributed among 150 owners: small men, tradesmen, provisioners, shipbuilders, and so on investing their savings. This activity provided a common overlap for almost every Shields trade—keelmen, dockers, provisioners, and sailmakers—and this was reinforced by interlocking insurance and broking clubs which formed a sort of unofficial town senate. Because of all this, admission to the town's elite (such as it was) was comparatively easy.

A further difference in Shields was the absence of work for women and children, which augmented family incomes in other towns. Hence the family income differential between, say, shipwrights and labourers stood out more sharply and the labour-force remained socially fragmented. In this situation, with no resident bourgeoisie, there was little scope for class formation.

Discussion of the three towns

In the early nineteenth century, and possibly in modern societies which have not fully developed the media of mass communication, people's idea of their society came mostly from their immediate community. While both South Shields and Northampton each had by the middle of the century less than a dozen men who would leave fortunes of over £25,000, Oldham had seventy and the fortunes of many of these were considerable. Furthermore, social mobility with the elite was much more restricted in Oldham. Engels had noted the importance of a 'resident bourgeoisie' in accounting for the different class reactions in Birmingham and Manchester. Much depends, as Weber also noted, on the 'transparency of the connection between the causes and the consequences of the class situation'. The problems which a historian faces in recreating such a situation are daunting and hence the importance of Foster's work.

The more typical reaction of the working class in later nineteenth-century provincial England was to withdraw from a confrontation with the total social success system by holding as their reference groups smaller subcultures with their own, more limited, versions of success. Thus, in order to avoid uncomfortable comparisons, members of each sub-group have to be *socially* similar with roughly the same job, income and way of life. The group's identity is then fixed in terms of the existing order; each group having its own 'pride' and its own 'respect'. The Shields sailors had their 'loyal standard'; late nineteenth-century Oldham clerks their paper-collar 'gentility'. Each group defined itself negatively, particularly against other groups with less good life chances.

Thus for a status group structure to crystallise into a class struggle much will depend on the local urban-industrial situation. More recent work on the inter-industry propensity to strike has brought together convincing evidence of the more strike-prone nature of isolated bodies of manual workers such as miners, deep-sea fishermen or dockers. Political sociologists have also noted more radical voting behaviour in more isolated communities in which manual workers are encapsulated from the dominant norms and values of the wider society. Foster also believes that where there are employment opportunities for women and children, semiskilled and unskilled manual workers were able to bring up the level of their family incomes, thus helping to overcome something of the subcultural distinctions. However, even if working-class subcultures can be coalesced, there still remains the problem of whether the subculture will remain basically 'respectful', or deferential, or whether it will demand a confrontation with ruling-class authority. It is here that the local urban-industrial system is crucial.

It is only fair to say that not all social and economic historians would accept Foster's analysis. Historians have their ideologies and values as much as anyone else and the story they tell will reflect these, directly or tacitly. 'The facts' do not speak for themselves as easily as some historians make out: they have to be selected and interpreted. But inevitably, historians will have to acquire the sociologists' theories of stratification and the sociologist will have to get used to handling unfamiliar data from unfamiliar sources. Only then will we get some real understanding of the *process* of urbanisation in Britain.

Inevitably, by selecting certain variables and situations for particular emphasis comprehensiveness may have to be sacrificed. Most historians have until recently been less than friendly, if not hostile, to Marxian historical sociology, presumably because of its political associations. However, Peter Laslett concludes his excellent introduction to sociological history *The World We Have Lost* (1965) by calling for a specifically sociological historical criticism. 'In such a new historical criticism the Marxian element in sociological thought because of its explanatory power will play a formidable part.'

TOWARDS A SOCIOLOGY OF URBANISATION IN BRITAIN

We have seen that the mere concentration of population within administrative areas, designated as urban, says little about the qualitative changes involved. Indeed, we have seen that many large cities are simply agglomerations of industrial villages. Furthermore, the response to urbanisation may vary widely. Between generalisation so broad as to be meaningless and the minutiae of the parish or ward's social history it is necessary to provide some kind of a framework, into which detailed local information may be fitted. We shall try to provide such a framework based on the important processes in this final section.

The migration process

(a) *The social structure of the area of emigration*. It is important to know whether the urban migrants came from *closed* villages, where at least half the acreage is owned by the squire himself in residence, or by an absentee landlord, or from *open* villages in which there are a significant proportion of peasants and freeholders. One would expect towns which largely recruited their populations mainly from one or the other type would differ markedly, peasants or freeholders being more independent-minded and more ready to seek radical solutions to the problems the urban situation thrust upon them.

(b) *The social structure of the receiving area*. We have already seen something of the variety as between Oldham, Northampton and South Shields. It is important to know whether migrants worked for one or a few employers in paternalist industrial villages, or whether they moved into large, speculatively-built urban estates. They may move into an established, even if rapidly growing, town with at least some facilities and social and political organisation, or they may move into a completely new town. Depending on the different occupational and industrial structures of the towns, so the response of the migrants to the urbanisation process will be different.

(*c*) *The nature of the links between areas of emigration and immigration.* Much depends on the actual physical distance the migrants have travelled. Where they have moved only a short distance they will be able to maintain kinship linkages with parents and siblings, who may have remained behind in the villages. Similarly, where people from a similar area move into a nearby town they are able to provide each other with social and economic support. This may take place as much with, say, Irish immigrants coming from a similar part of Ireland and settling together in a quarter of an English town, or for local migrants from nearby villages. The social controls and cultural patterns of the previous milieu may be maintained, transformed or developed in the new situation.

(*d*) *The age/sex balance of the migrating population.* Sometimes a town may grow gradually so that its age structure may be reasonably balanced. In other cases all the migrants may be young men and women in their twenties and thirties with young children, who of course will all grow old together leading to a bulge moving through the age pyramid. In towns where there is a high demand for male employment with very little for women and children it may be that the immigrant population has a very unbalanced sex structure. The temporary preponderance of men may on the one hand lead to vice, drunkenness and prostitution; alternatively, the lack of alternative employment may lead to poverty and overcrowding, as people are obliged to share dwellings to minimise the cost of rent. However, this point should not be over stressed. The strong demand for female domestic servants served not only to balance the sex-ratio but also, in some cases, to unbalance in the opposite direction so that men were heavily outnumbered for a time.

Encapsulation or assimilation

(*a*) *Industrial villages.* If countrymen from the surrounding area move in, bringing their pigs to keep in their backyards, and are surrounded

by friends and kin from their area of origin, then they may stay encapsulated within the urban system for a hundred years or more.
There need be no sharp break in primary or secondary group ties;
houses may be owned and retained in the family; jobs may be found
for their children when they are old enough and later they may marry
and settle down in their own or one of the neighbouring urban-
industrial villages. Despite the census evidence there would not be
any great change in their way of living as a result of urbanisation.
Some of the more rural customs will decline to be sure, but the
break will not be traumatic and vestiges of the earlier culture will
linger on for many years, as recent radio documentaries based on
tape-recorded interviews with the oldest inhabitants of Northampton
and Ipswich illustrated so vividly. Stella Davies's book *North Country
Bred* is well worth reading in this context. However, here again it is
worth remembering that none of this would apply for the more
mobile workers. We must be very cautious about how much we can
generalise from the particular.

(*b*) *Assimilation by association.* Social historians emphasise the
plethora of voluntary associations during the early period of urbanisation in Britain. Some of these were basic instrumental activities, for
example, the forms of forced savings such as the Benefit or Friendly
societies, being collective responses to individual crises and problems.
These voluntary organisations were a direct response to urbanism
and were, as the Hammonds put it, 'the defences of the poor', in
their book on *The Town Labourer*.

The man who has no share in the government of his parish or mill needs
some scope for his political capacities; the man who spends his life 'making the twenty-fourth part of a pin' needs some sphere for his imagination;
the man whose only provision against accident or illness or the loss of his
livelihood is the reluctant succour of the poor law, needs some protection
against fortune; the man who lives under the unbridled power of employer and magistrate needs some protection against that power, some
pledge of help and friendship in the hour of struggle and tribulation. These
necessaries of his larger life the English workman sought during the
Industrial Revolution in organisations that he created and developed under
the fierce discouragement of his rulers.

Documentation of these voluntary associations is available in many of the standard social histories.

(c) *From the urban village to the urban system.* The voluntary association very often served as a bridge between the individual's local system of industrial village or segregated occupation or craft to the wider urban society. However, it was only when men saw the situation in larger terms, and became aware of their class position in the wider society, that they may be said to be truly urbanised. Hence a large proportion of the population in the nineteenth century was urbanised in the demographic sense but had not yet moved into the urban system to be urbanised in the sociological sense. They were in the city but not of it. This is an important distinction and hence the relevance of Foster's work on class formation discussed above. If Northampton shoe-makers were still operating with rural reference groups—that is if they were comparing their lot favourably with friends and kin in the villages they had left—then their meaningful social world was not yet the town. The switching of reference groups and the restructuring of normative behaviour to the large-scale society should be the essential focus of a sociological approach to urbanisation.

This somewhat terse and categorical statement on the nature of the process of urbanisation does considerably less than justice to a large and complex literature. Most recent studies are concerned with urbanisation in the contemporary world and it is possible to make some very illuminating comparisons and contrasts between nineteenth-century Britain and mid-twentieth century Africa or Latin America. For those who may feel stimulated to make these connections for themselves I have included some references in the list for this chapter.

Urbanisation and the family

In 1845 Frederick Engels published a vigorous attack on the urban-industrial system: *The Condition of the Working Class in England.* Leaving aside the polemics, however understandable in the contemporary situation, Engels's work is still one of the most perceptive accounts of urban social conditions and the section on 'The Great Towns' is based on personal fieldwork as well as documentary and statistical analysis, particularly on the city of Manchester. He argues, with most other Victorian social reformers, that the appalling physical conditions in the great industrial cities were having severe effects on the health, physique and moral and social relationships of the working population. Historians do not all accept the typicality or extent of the conditions described in contemporary reports of the early nineteenth century but certainly parts of such cities as Leeds, Liverpool, Glasgow, and Manchester were as foul as the most lurid descriptions portray. It was in this context that Engels wrote:

Thus the social order makes family life almost impossible for the worker. In a comfortless, filthy house, hardly good enough for mere nightly shelter, ill-furnished, often neither rain-tight nor warm, a foul atmosphere filling rooms overcrowded with human beings, no domestic comfort is possible. The husband works the whole day through, perhaps the wife also and the elder children, all in different places; they meet night and morning only, all under perpetual temptation to drink; what family life is possible under such conditions?

Clearly one needs to know how general such conditions were. In Oldham two related families at different stages in their life cycle would combine to form one household. A husband and wife with young children would live with their parents, being supported by them and by unmarried siblings while their own children were under the age of eight or nine, and then later on when their children went out to work they would repay their parents by then supporting them. This huddling together of the impoverished working class varied between towns and over time. Overcrowding would be matched by a large number of empty houses, which would be inhabited or not depending on local economic fluctuations. The proportion of households in Oldham in 1851 containing three generations, and sometimes also siblings and related families of the same generation, was 21 per cent. In Northampton the figure was 14 per cent and Shields 11 per cent.

Certainly in some parts of some cities primary group relationships, particularly the family, were less stable, and symptoms of social dis-organisation such as drunkenness and vice are well-documented. Often such conditions were very short-lived, associated with the rapid immigration of young unmarried men, presenting the same kinds of problems as appear today in African mining towns.

Any attempt to make qualitative judgments about the nature of family life at different historical periods and under different economic conditions is an extremely hazardous exercise. However, as Peter Laslett (1965) emphasises: 'It remains the case that there slept together under each roof in 1600 only the nuclear family, with the addition of servants where necessary. Therefore in that vital respect one's ancestors were not different from ourselves. They were the same.' Laslett's book is essential reading for demythologising the past. The 'normal' state of affairs in preindustrial England was for the parents and children of the nuclear family to live separately, with extra-familial kin living in the vicinity. For a time, in some cities, a proportion—probably a minority—of families shared the same living arrangements with extra-familial kin. This so-called 'extended' family household was not any kind of typical pattern: paradoxically, urban-industrialism had the effect of *over*emphasising family rela-tionships as a form of defence and security. Hence to talk today about a 'decline' in the 'extended' family is a curious sort of nonsense. For a certain section of the population over a limited period of time linkages with extra-familial kin were overstressed. As the system settled down the dominance of the nuclear family reasserted itself.

Hence Engels's statement about the family is most misleading. There is an implicit assumption that housing conditions in rural areas were necessarily better and there is a lot of evidence to the con-trary. Further, he implies that the quality of a relationship depends on length of face-to-face contact. If that were the case, we should be equally concerned about present-day long-distance commuters to the city of London who are away from the house for eleven or twelve hours, and whose children are at boarding school. The problems of the working class under the conditions of early urban-industrialism were acute and in many respects similar to those in the rapidly grow-ing cities of Latin America, Asia, and Africa today. Like presentday urbanising peasants their response to this situation varied, but the most remarkable thing, surely, is the strength of the family to adjust and adapt to the demands put upon it.

Social structure and spatial structure I—The socio-geographic pattern

ECOLOGY AND THE CHICAGO SCHOOL OF URBAN SCOIOLOGY
Many of the terms used to describe the socio-spatial structure of
urban areas were first used by urban sociologists at the University of
Chicago in the interwar period (Park, *et al.*, 1925). Cities were described as having a characteristic structure and patterns of growth
said to have general application. E. W. Burgess, for example, described Chicago in terms of a series of concentric zones having distinctive social and physical characteristics, which, he claimed, might
be generally true for all cities (see fig. 1). Other research workers emphasised the wedgelike character of urban growth or the multiple
nuclei structure, with each nucleus having a distinctive function or
social character.

The Chicago School of urban sociology also investigated the so-
called 'natural areas' of cities which together formed 'a mosaic of
little worlds which touch but do not inter-penetrate', in R. E. Park's
phrase. This segregation was seen as a physical fact reinforcing social
distance, with each area having its own subcultural values and contributing to the 'natural' life of the city. The processes which produce these segregated or 'natural' areas were partly social and partly
subsocial. Park sought to understand the sifting and sorting mechanisms which 'select' appropriate individuals to live in appropriate
areas: ultimately, he said, it is *competition*—the struggle for space—
which allocates people to their position in society and their position
in space. The division of labour involves 'competitive cooperation'
and, borrowing heavily from ecology, Park described society in
terms of symbiotic relationships (Park, 1952).

Those in the most 'dominant' position controlled the most valuable part of the city—the central business district (C.B.D.) Next to this is the zone in transition, which, at the time when the Chicago sociologists were doing their studies, was a colourful and varied area of slums, bohemia, immigrant ghettoes, rented rooms and so on. Clearly

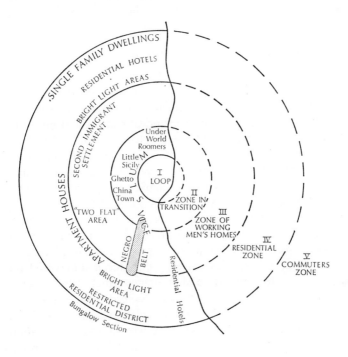

Fig. 1   Burgess' Diagram of City Ecology.

they were concerned with a particular city at a particular period of time with a given technology, so that their understanding of the processes of growth and change was not always very clear. The zone of transition presumably had different social characteristics in the past and would have different social characteristics in the future. Not all receive successive waves of immigrants who 'invade' certain areas cities leading to 'dominance' and ultimately 'succession' of the new element. According to this ecological approach, people are gripped by a kind of economic determinism over which they have little or no control. Contemporary urban sociologists accept the importance of social ecology as a valuable descriptive tool but reject the sub-social ecological framework on which much of the early work was based (see Morris, 1958).

SPATIAL STRUCTURE IN HISTORICAL PERSPECTIVE

Before considering some recent analyses of British cities, based on census information, it is instructive to consider British urban spatial structure in perspective. The peculiar characteristics of urbanism in this country need to be seen in historical context and most of our towns and cities retain many spatial characteristics relating to an earlier period of growth. Unlike American cities, European cities have grown and developed from medieval origins and this has important implications for the socio-economic pattern today. Hence, although British towns have their C.B.D.s they also have their cathedrals, castles and physical remains of other medieval institutions. Such features are symbols of other value systems which may or may not reinforce the system based on profits and rents. Generally of course the lay or ecclesiastical elite introduced differential rents, charging more for property and frontages which were better protected or more accessible to customers. Nevertheless, economic competition did not produce the kind of ecological segregation which is more characteristic of modern cities. There was some segregation by trade or craft, so that towns developed distinctive functional areas, but rich and poor were not so sharply separated in a physical sense, partly because medieval cities were smaller than their modern counterparts.

This lack of segregation before the seventeenth century may be partly explained by the relatively slow rate of population growth and the difficulties of extending the existing built-up areas. The town's political privileges related to a limited area which it was difficult for it to extend. Hence, urban densities increased at the expense of social segregation. Small cottages were squeezed between more substantial houses and rich merchants, unable to get land at the periphery, even if they wanted it, were obliged to build high on existing central city plots. Medieval suburbs were as socially mixed and as physically heterogeneous as the centres. Admittedly certain sites attracted higher values—for example merchants clustered in the fashionable Radcliffe area of Bristol in order to get river frontages to their gardens—but other merchants in that city would rather live in towers built upon the city walls than have a long journey to work. Privacy did not seem to be highly valued.

CONTRAST BETWEEN PROVINCIAL AND METROPOLITAN SPATIAL STRUCTURES

One of the most distinctive features of English urbanism is the contrast between London and the provincial cities. The metropolis developed a distinctive social and spatial structure not matched by other English towns. As early as the sixteenth century historians noted the polarisation between the industrial and impoverished area east of the city and the wealthy area stretching westwards to Westminster and the Court. In 1662 Petty remarked on the 'pallaces of the greatest men' in the west as those escaping from the 'fumes steams and stinks of the whole easterly pyle' left the old great houses of the City which then became halls for companies or were turned into tenements. This polarisation became even more acute towards the end of the seventeenth century when new, planned, residential development in the west, coupled with the rapid expansion of population, drew the rich and poor further apart. The implications of this spatial segregation for social policy was seen clearly by Colquhoun, a police magistrate for the Tower Hamlets, who described the situation in 1797.

The lower classes [in the eastern parishes] . . . are compelled to contribute largely to the fund for supporting the poor from the daily pittance which arises from labour . . . while in almost every other part of the metropolis, as the rich form a considerable proportion of the inhabitants . . . the burden does not attach. And thus it happens that in Spitalfields and Mile End New Town from five shillings in the pound are paid ... and after all extremely inadequate to the wants of the poor, while St George's Hanover Square and St Marylebone paying only two shillings to two and sixpence in the pound, and the poor are abundantly fed, while the labouring poor in that part of the town are eased of a heavy burden (quoted in George, 1965 p. 332n).

This overall polarisation, which emerged between the sixteenth century and the eighteenth, was superimposed on a polynuclear pattern more typical of the preindustrial city. London was divided into Park's 'mosaic of little worlds', partly because of difficulties of communication, partly because of rigid lines of demarcation between trades and occupations and partly because of the local government structure. However, Mrs George, the historian of *London Life in the Eighteenth Century*, claims that by the beginning of her period the distinctiveness of the small localities had been lessened.

Unfortunately there has been very little systematic historical urban sociology and we have to be content with the assertions of historians, based on partial evidence. It is possible that this situation will be remedied to some degree by the researches of the Cambridge group of historical demographers, who hope to use certain series of parish registers to provide precise empirical evidence of social and economic changes in specific areas over a 300-year period.

SEGREGATION AS A FUNCTION OF POPULATION
CONCENTRATION AND INCREASE, AND SOCIAL MOBILITY

The enormous expansion of urban populations in the nineteenth century created new and distinctive patterns of urbanism. The concentration of the labour force in factories led to the rapid development of estates of cheap working men's cottages built as closely as possible to the centres of employment. The rise of the new middle class, based on the growth of manufacturing industry, produced new housing demands quite out of scale with the previous situation in provincial towns. The horse-drawn tram and later the railways helped to carry the middle class away from the working class. As industrialism and economic growth produced its new and expanding class structure, so people increasingly sought to make clear by where they lived, their position in the social structure. People who are sure of their position in society may be less afraid to live near those of lower status. As social mobility increases so place of residence becomes increasingly important as a means of buying and establishing a position in society.

SOCIO-GEOGRAPHIC PATTERNS IN A HISTORIC ENGLISH CITY

It is only by systematic analysis of census material that a detailed picture of the socio-geographic patterns of contemporary cities can be drawn. Oxford is one of the few English cities which has been carefully analysed, being the first place for which information was made available for small areas of about 3,000 people having similar social and economic characteristics. The pattern of residential development in Oxford has spread out in wedges from the centre for a variety of local historical and geographical reasons. The distribution of the social classes within each sector shows interesting variations. For example, social class I, the professional workers, are heavily overrepresented in the northern sector, comprising 11·7 per cent of the population of that sector in 1951. On the other hand, professional workers avoided the south-east, south and west sectors comprising only 2·7, 2·6, and 3·8 per cent of these sectors respectively (Collison and Mogey, 1959).

Not only are there differences according to sector, but also according to distance from the town centre. The city was divided into three zones, the first being within a radius of a mile from the centre, the second between a mile and two miles' radius and the third stretches from a circle of two miles' radius to the city boundary. It was found that the proportions of social class I and II decrease in moving further from the city centre, whereas class III containing the skilled manual workers *increased*. On the other hand, classes IV and V, the semi and unskilled occupations, followed the pattern of classes I and

II being most heavily concentrated at the centre. When sectors and zones were combined together, the concentration of classes I and II towards the centre and in the north became even more marked: in the northern first mile sector-zone just over a half of the population was in class I or class II, as opposed to only 13·6 per cent in the southern first mile sector zone.

Of course, none of this is at all surprising for anyone who knows Oxford. The University and buildings of architectural distinction are in the centre and the factories are at the periphery. In 1951 St Ebbes in south Oxford was a slum area, whereas north Oxford had been developed in the late nineteenth and early twentieth centuries with substantial homes for dons, following the decision to allow college Fellows to marry. Furthermore, the city housing policy has resulted in local authority housing estates being built at the edge of the city, leading to further deviation from the simple zonal hypothesis outlined by Burgess, which postulated richer commuters living at the periphery. This necessary segregation of municipal from private housing reinforced the segregation of classes I and II from the rest but reduced the segregation of classes III, IV, and V. Segregation is measured by an index which, in effect, is the percentage of the groups in question which would have to move elsewhere in order for there to be no significant difference in residential pattern.

At a finer level of analysis it was shown that terminal education age was the most significant indicator of residential segregation (Collison, 1960). Those whose education ended at age fifteen were the least segregated, whereas those whose education continued to age twenty-one or twenty-two were the most segregated. On the other hand those whose education ended at fourteen were also sharply segregated, showing a relatively high concentration in areas of poor housing. The amount of residential dissimilarity was greater between categories whose education ended above the age of seventeen than those below. Thus there are indications that each year of education which is received after the age of seventeen has a greater effect on residential location than each year of education received before it. This Oxford study demonstrates the difficulties in making the Chicago theories of urban spatial structure have general validity.

SOCIO-GEOGRAPHIC PATTERNS IN A NEW TOWN

The New Town of Crawley in Sussex is divided into nine neighbour-hoods ringing the town centre in two bands. These neighbourhoods are separated from each other by roads, railways or open spaces and differ markedly from each other in social composition. For example, the proportion of class I ranges from 8·1 per cent in Gossops Green to 1·4 per cent in Langley Green. Such differences are related to the pattern of growth of the town and the class composition of immi-grants at different periods, and also to the movements of population within the town. As the New Town grew so the pattern of labour requirements changed: workers in the manufacturing industries were needed in the early days, whereas more professional people were needed later on. Inevitably, new arrivals were allocated houses in the neighbourhoods then being built (Heraud, 1968).

There is also substantial movement within the town, particularly from subsidised to unsubsidised dwellings. An analysis of households leaving Development Corporation tenancies between 1956 and 1959 showed that the proportion of movers in classes I and II was double that of the proportion of these classes in Crawley as a whole (Heraud, 1968). Of course many of these moved out of the town altogether to houses in the surrounding towns and villages. The effect of this internal population turbulence and emigration has been to produce an inner ring of more predominantly working-class housing, sur-rounded by the later-built and more middle-class neighbourhoods. The Development Corporation has aided this pattern by the siting of unsubsidised housing for lease or for sale.

In an analysis of degrees of segregation of the five social classes it was found that the extent of segregation in Crawley in 1961 was less than in Oxford in 1951. There were, however, some interesting dif-ferences: class III, the skilled workers, appeared to be less segregated in Crawley in 1961 than in Oxford in 1951, perhaps reflecting a greater affluence or changed status for this category. However, great care must be taken in coming to such conclusions, since class V, the unskilled category, also appears to be less segregated from class II and class III. One of the reasons for these differences between

43

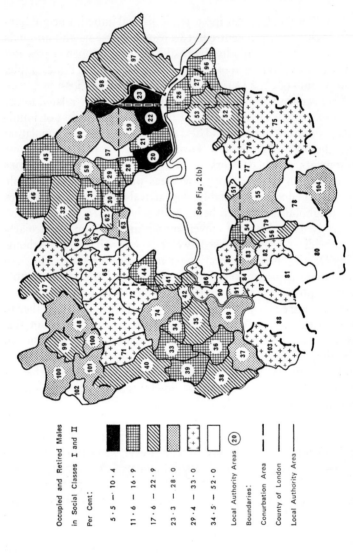

Occupied and Retired Males
in Social Classes I and II
Per Cent:

5·5 — 10·4
11·6 — 16·9
17·6 — 22·9
23·3 — 28·0
29·4 — 33·0
34·5 — 52·0

⟨20⟩ Local Authority Areas

Boundaries:

Conurbation Area
County of London
Local Authority Area

Fig. 2(a) Social Class in Greater London, 1951.

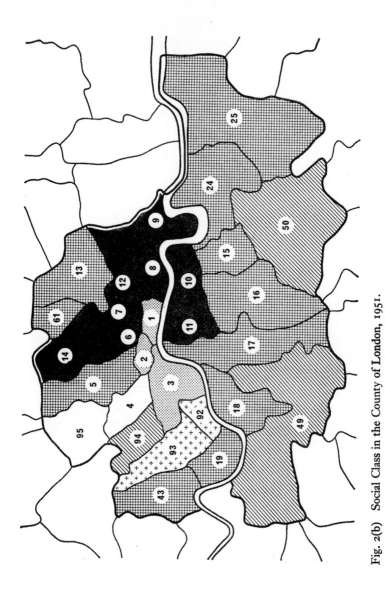

Fig. 2(b)   Social Class in the County of London, 1951.

1. City of London
2. Holborn
3. Westminster
4. St. Marylebone
5. St. Pancras
6. Finsbury
7. Shoreditch
8. Stepney
9. Poplar
10. Bermondsey
11. Southwark
12. Bethnal Green
13. Hackney
14. Islington
15. Deptford
16. Camberwell
17. Lambeth
18. Battersea
19. Fulham
20. West Ham C.B.
21. East Ham C.B.
22. Barking
23. Dagenham
24. Greenwich
25. Woolwich
26. Erith
27. Crayford
28. Leyton
29. Walthamstow
30. Tottenham
31. Edmonton
32. Enfield
33. Hayes & Harlington
34. Southall
35. Heston & Isleworth
36. Feltham

37. Sunbury
38. Staines
39. Yiewsley & West Drayton
40. Uxbridge
41. Acton
42. Brentford & Chiswick
43. Hammersmith
44. Willesden
45. Waltham Holy Cross
46. Cheshunt
47. Elstree
48. Bushey
49. Wandsworth
50. Lewisham
51. Penge
52. Chislehurst & Sidcup
53. Bexley
54. Mitcham
55. Croydon C.B.
56. Carshalton
57. Wanstead & Woodford
58. Chingford
59. Ilford
60. Chigwell
61. Stoke Newington
62. Wood Green
63. Hornsey
64. Finchley
65. Hendon
66. Southgate
67. Friern Barnet
68. East Barnet
69. Barnet
70. Potter's Bar
71. Ruislip-Northwood
72. Wembley

73. Harrow
74. Ealing
75. Orpington
76. Bromley
77. Beckenham
78. Coulsdon & Purley
79. Beddington & Wallington
80. Banstead
81. Epsom & Ewell
82. Sutton & Cheam
83. Merton & Morden
84. Malden & Coombe
85. Wimbledon
86. Barnes
87. Surbiton
88. Esher
89. Twickenham
90. Richmond
91. Kingston
92. Chelsea
93. Kensington
94. Paddington
95. Hampstead

Areas Outside Census Conurbation, but included in Royal Commission Review Area

96. Dartford M.B.
97. Hornchurch
98. Romford
99. Watford M.B.
100. Watford R.D.
101. Rickmansworth
102. Chorley Wood
103. Walton & Weybridge
104. Caterham & Warlingham

Fig. 2(c) List of Local Authority Areas in and Around the Conurbation of Greater London, before the Reorganisation of Local Government.

Crawley and Oxford may be that dwellings at different rents for different categories are built in clusters and are not scattered through the neighbourhoods. Thus small enclaves of 'deviant' class categories may exist, which need a finer level of analysis to reveal.

TABLE 4

Indices of segregation Oxford 1951 *and Crawley* 1961

Social class	Oxford 1951	Crawley 1961
I Professional	35	17
II Intermediate professional	25	17
III Skilled manual and unskilled non-manual	13	6
IV Semiskilled	8	22
V Unskilled	18	13

Source: Heraud, 1968, Tables 6 and 7.

It is clear therefore that discussions about 'socially mixed' populations, or the class balance in New Towns, depends very much on the level of analysis. The town as a whole may reflect the national class structure fairly accurately, but at a local or neighbourhood level patterns of segregation may remain sharp. Not only do neighbourhoods differ from each other in social composition but also neighbourhoods will reveal a greater or lesser degree of segregation within themselves, depending on the policy of the Development Corporation in providing houses for sale or at unsubsidised rents.

THE SOCIO-GEOGRAPHIC PATTERN OF THE METROPOLIS

Charles Booth, in his classic survey of the labour and life of the people of London at the end of the nineteenth century, commented on south London: 'This population . . . is found to be poorer ring by ring as the centre is approached. . . . While at its very heart . . . there exists a very impenetrable mass of poverty.' This is still largely applicable today.

Research at the Centre for Urban Studies, at University College, London, has documented the changing structure of Greater London

47

(Westergaard, 1964). Using such criteria as class composition, the net balance of inward and outward movements to work and the degree of dependence on employment in Central London, sixteen socio-geographic zones have been distinguished (see fig. 2). Surrounding the central employment zone, which has a day population of about a million more than the night population, is a broad belt of working-class housing stretching from Fulham, Battersea, and Lambeth, south of the Thames through Southwark and Bermondsey to Shoreditch, with extension through Bethnal Green and Hackney to Islington. To the west of the centre there is a zone of very mixed social character; in Chelsea and Kensington about a third of the occupied and retired males are in social classes I and II, but high-class residential areas mingle with lodging house areas and long-established pockets of poverty. The proportion in social classes I and II drops on moving north into Paddington, but increases to between a third and a half of the total population in Hampstead.

The main middle-class areas in the south, from Orpington through Banstead to Epsom and Esher, are separated by the working-class East End and the industrial areas of West London—Acton, Hammersmith and Willesden—from the north-west middle-class suburbs stretching from Wembley and Harrow through Hendon to Barnet and Potters Bar. A further industrial belt stretching up the Lea Valley separates the north-west middle-class suburbs from the north-east middle-class suburbs of Woodford, Chingford and Chigwell.

Certainly there is something of a concentric pattern in the social-class map of Greater London, despite the extension of industrial belts to the west and up the Lea Valley. However, new public housing built over the past twenty years has enabled or obliged more working-class people to live further out.

There are also interesting variations in age structure in Greater London, and these to some extent follow the same territorial patterns as those revealed by variation in social class. For example, working-class areas generally have higher rates of fertility and mortality, thus having a younger population than the middle-class areas. But there are also differences between the inner and outer suburbs, irrespective of their social composition, the younger families with children being drawn further outwards to the newer suburbs. The proportion of children under fifteen years old ranging from roughly one in ten in central areas to one in four in the outer suburbs. Of course a large proportion of local authority areas show no great deviation in age structure from the average, but analysis of the remainder has revealed five types. The following account is based on Westergaard's analysis of the 1951 census data (Westergaard, 1964).

1. *The Central and West End Type*

This type characteristically has a very high proportion of young people aged 20–24—between 30 and 40 per cent above the Greater London average—and a very low proportion of young children—in the case of Westminster 40 per cent less than the Greater London average. Such extreme variations in age structure are, of course, exceptional and are found in the City, Holborn or Westminster. However, Chelsea, Kensington, and Hampstead show a similar pattern, although to a less marked extent.

2. *Old-established 'middle-ring' middle-class suburbs*

In districts of this type the relatively low fertility and low mortality of a mainly middle-class population accounts for a characteristically high proportion of elderly people—between 30 and 40 per cent and above the Greater London average in the case of Wimbledon for those aged sixty-five and over in 1951—and a rather small proportion of children—again in the case of Wimbledon the proportion of those aged fifteen to nineteen is 20 per cent below the Greater London average.

3. *Inner working-class districts*

In these areas the proportionately higher mortality and fertility brings the proportion of young people some 10 to 20 per cent above and the proportion of those over thirty-five some 10 to 20 per cent below the Greater London average. Of course redevelopment and rehousing can radically alter this pattern within a very few years as young people with children move further out, leaving the more elderly behind. However, the general pattern is applicable to the inner working-class areas, particularly those of East London.

4. *Outer middle-class suburbs*

This type is characteristically found in new suburbs at the edge of the conurbation having a higher proportion of children and young people under twenty and adults some twenty to thirty years older. The proportions of young adults between twenty and thirty years or elderly people over fifty-five is below the greater London average.

5. *Outer working-class suburbs*

As with type 4 there can be wide fluctuations within this type depending on how far the 'bulge' of high fertility at the time of settlement has moved through the age structure. Some districts will have a double bulge, arising from the higher fertility and lower age of marriage of a well-established working-class population provided with local employment.

A number of important points need to be remembered when considering this typology. First, those areas which show little deviation from this average will change over time. Thus areas in type 4 may move out of the typology for a period before reappearing as type 2. New suburbs at the periphery or beyond the Green Belt in the Outer Metropolitan Area then come into type 4. Secondly, not only does the actually physical situation of the different types change but also at any one time the areas grouped together do not necessarily form zones. Paradoxically the type that remains most stable physically— the centre and West End is socially the most unstable. The characteristics remain the same even though the actual population is constantly changing. The zone of transition may thus be more stable over time, in terms of its demographic structure, than are most suburbs.

MORE RECENT WORK IN THE IDENTIFICATION OF URBAN SUB-AREAS

The 1961 Census provides more detailed information than had previously been available, since data was gathered and processed on the basis of much smaller units known as enumeration districts. One study by Elizabeth Gittus (1965) analysed 1,800 enumeration districts in Merseyside and 1,700 in Hampshire and these were classified according to the combined evidence of sixty indices. They included the proportion of the population who were of school age, born overseas, living in overcrowded conditions; the proportion of households in shared dwellings, with just one or two members, having exclusive use of certain household amenities, renting their accommodation from the local authority; the proportion of dwellings in multistorey buildings, or with no fixed bath installed and an approximate measure of fertility in the ratio of the number of children under five to the number of women of child-bearing age. Research workers at the University of Liverpool then attempted to assess which indicators provided the greatest proportion of variation between enumeration districts by the somewhat complicated statistical exercise of component analysis. It was found that the most basic indicator of variation between different areas in a city was persons per room and this was almost as important in Hampshire as in Merseyside where a quarter of the total variation between districts was accounted for by this index.

CONCLUDING DISCUSSION

It would be possible to present evidence demonstrating that certain characteristics of a given urban population such as religious affiliation, voting behaviour, skin colour and so on are not spread randomly throughout an urban area. These and many other characteristics cluster together to a greater or lesser extent and sociologists are interested in the way these patterns of segregation become more or less marked. We have been mainly concerned with the distribution of social class and age structure characteristics since these patterns are often closely associated with other less important characteristics.

However, it is important that the limitations of a concept such as segregation are understood. An assymetrical distribution of three people could, according to one definition, be described as segregation; the functional differentiation of medieval cities according to trade or craft could also be described as one sort of segregation. Interest and research in urban social segregation may seem to be in direct proportion to the amount of detailed census information available. In this chapter we have shifted the level of discussion between broad intuitive statements about segregation by contemporaries in Elizabethan London to careful statistical manipulation of small census tract or enumeration district data. The mesh of the net has got finer but this does not necessarily imply a better *understanding* of the relationships between social structure and spatial structure. Our descriptive devices may have improved but there is a danger that too great a concern with techniques will be at the expense of understanding or explanation.

Clearly there will be different patterns of segregation between towns, and over time within towns, depending on the nature and scale of the growth and change of population. Depending on the industrial and occupational structure of a given town there will be a greater or lesser spread of incomes and therefore, presumably, of house types. In places such as Dagenham, Bootle or Rhondda the population is almost entirely composed of manual workers, whereas places such as Coulsdon or Beckenham have only about 10 per cent of their populations in social classes IV and V. Similarly towns which grow rapidly over a short period of time, associated with the growth or expansion of a specific industry, will inevitably have large areas of housing of about the same date and type, tending to a segregation of population with certain characteristics.

The most interesting questions are associated with *change*. The sociogeographic pattern of a city at any one point of time is certainly of some interest. However, a comparison of different patterns over a period of time raises more interesting sociological questions. Partly, of course, these different patterns are due to the fact that the physical buildings age and hence become more or less desirable. Housing once appropriate for an affluent middle class may, over time, with changing standards and social patterns, become converted into overcrowded flats for the poor. It is these questions of growth and change which oblige us to move from socio-geographical description to sociological analysis, to which we turn in the next chapter.

Social structure and spatial structure II—Housing classes and the socio-ecological system

CONSTRAINTS

In the last chapter we saw that the population of urban areas was typically segregated according to various characteristics, of which type of occupation and education were the most important. In this chapter we shall examine some of the sociological processes inherent in the patterns. Using certain characteristics as indices of categories of the population, it is clear that these categories cluster and are not spread randomly throughout the urban areas. Thus we must assume that people are distributed more as a result of the *constraints* that operate upon them in the choices they make, rather than being distributed simply according to *chance*. There is a reciprocal relationship between the social structure and the spatial structure, between physical distance and social distance. Segregation of the poor in slums, for example, will have different sociological consequences from their being scattered more randomly throughout the urban area.

Clearly everyone is constrained to a greater or lesser degree. Urban sociologists are concerned with the basic constraints which affect people's life chances in urban areas, in so far as these fall into a pattern. We will discuss some of these constraints by making them analytically distinct, although of course, they tend to reinforce one another.

Economic constraints

The occupational structure rewards differentially: families take their position in the social structure by the amount of reward—power, wealth, prestige, security, and so on—which the economic system allocates to the chief earner. Those who may expect regular increments of salary and have high job security thereby gain access to capital, through bank loans and mortgages; those who are paid very highly gain power, since they gain access to scarce resources; while those with little occupational security, employed in declining industries or with a cyclical or a periodic pattern of work are less likely to have access to capital and will not have much power in the struggle for scarce resources. Thus people's position in the occupational structure to a large degree determines their position within the urban system.

Theoretically, and operating with a model of rational economic man, one would expect those with most power to reinforce their position by taking the physically most advantageous positions within the urban system. The spatial structure would then be a direct reflection of the distribution of power in society. The rich would have the choice of whether they lived in the centre of cities, where land values are highest and access to facilities is greatest; or they could use their wealth to control or buy the means of mobility so that they may travel some distance to work and facilities.

With this simple model the poor would find themselves doubly disadvantaged: they would get fewer rewards from the economic system anyway and they would have to pay a higher proportion of their income to get the same facilities as the rich. Now, since anything short of a random scatter of the population inevitably involves an inequitable distribution of facilities, the unequal rewards from the occupational system create acute deprivation for a minority and relative deprivation, in terms of access to some facilities, for almost all.

We saw in the last chapter that the rich or most powerful exercise their choice to their own best advantage. In the case of Oxford, and similar old-established cities, the rich live in the centre or near to it, close to the social and physical amenities which are there. Where there are factories, gasworks, railway goods yards and so on in the centre, the advantage of easy access to facilities becomes offset by the dirt, noise, and smells produced by these features. The poor live near the centre or in the east, the rich move out to the west where generally the prevailing wind carries the smoke and dirt away from them.

Social constraints

For some people a house is simply a shelter; for others it is a position in society. A house may be a physical symbol of one's position in the social structure. Dr Chapman in his book *The Home and Social Status* (1955) has demonstrated very clearly how the physical appearance and furnishings of a home are directly related to the social status of those living there. Even within local authority housing estates, where there may be very little variation in rents, certain areas acquire a reputation for being 'respectable' and others are 'rough'. In Kuper's (1953) study of a cul-de-sac in a new council estate just outside Coventry one family in three moved in a period of less than four years. A high proportion of these moves were for status reasons; some moved to 'a better area' others moved to a 'friendlier' area. 'In this cul-de-sac, respectability and roughness tend to have a territorial basis. The direction of change is towards increasing "roughness", which we think can also be seen in the lower standards of care lavished on the front door steps and in litter on the open forecourts' (p. 148). Those at the margin between the 'working'and the 'middle' class are more likely to be aware of the importance of their physical situation. W. G. Runciman (1966, pp. 239–40), discusses the attitudes of manual workers rating themselves as middle class. He found that a fifth of all those who wanted to move from their present district did so because of the kind of area it was. The proportion for the highest-paid group was 27 per cent.

Finally, those in the middle class, whose career provides them with increasing increments, may be able to change their residence as they change their status in an occupational hierarchy. Where promotion involves geographical mobility, such people may use their extra earnings to buy an appropriate slot in the urban system. New estates are advertised in terms of the 'sort of people' who are going to live there, and estate agents help to fit prospective purchasers into what they consider to be the socially most appropriate house and

3

area. Of course, it is those who are socially mobile who are most in need of taking their social cues from others, and reference groups or patterns of normative behaviour are not as fluid as this for the majority of the British population.

Perhaps we might illustrate the economic and social constraints by following Runciman and envisaging two forms of Utopia. In the first form of Utopia there is equality of economic reward but not of social evaluation: that is, although everyone is paid the same economic reward for his work, different occupations are allocated different prestige, so that it is still, for example, 'better' to be a professional worker than a clerk, or a skilled worker than an unskilled worker. Under these conditions, with the inevitable division of labour, and even with identical houses for all, marked segregation by occupation might appear, with distinct and separate styles of life in these physically similar but socially distinct areas.

In the second type of Utopia there is equality of social evaluation but inequality of economic reward: that is, there is a wide discrepancy between the economic reward paid to, say, a university professor compared with a university cleaner, but they treat each other in a spirit of mutual respect and equality. Given the ready availability of building land in appropriate sites, there may be wide variety of house types of different sizes and quality of building, but these are not segregated by status criteria and may be distributed in an urban area according to other criteria, such as nearness to work (so that the university professor and university cleaner may live next door to one another). In such a society the ecological models and quantitative techniques, which imply a non-random scatter of the population, would have to be modified. Certainly these methods might still be used, possibly to demonstrate segregation by industrial (as opposed to occupational) structure.

People are also constrained by their age, sex, marital status, family relationships, and social networks. We will return to these variables later.

Spatial constraints and access to facilities
Men who are paid the same wage, have exactly the same conditions

of work, and exactly the same aspirations and reference group perspectives, may nevertheless have very different patterns of behaviour depending on whether they live close to their work and other facilities. Studies in France (Chombart de Lauwe, *et al.*, 1960) have analysed the time budgets of carefully matched groups of workers, and it is clear that time spent playing with children and hence the children's relationships with their parents, the conjugal relationship, the amount of leisure time and so on are all directly affected by the length of the journey to work. Hence one can hold the economic and social constraints constant and analyse the distinctive constraints imposed by the distribution of jobs, schools, health facilities, shops, recreational facilities and so on. The spatial logic of location theory may determine the size of settlement in which an individual finds himself. This in turn will provide him with a given range of employment, housing choice and so on. On the other hand, certain types of employment may only be found in certain types of settlements. Depending on the individual's position in the social structure, so he will be more or less able to accommodate himself to these constraints. Capital or certain types of job may be necessary to get a house elsewhere, low income may make a long journey to work impossible and so on.

Take two men living in different parts of the country, getting the same nationally negotiated wage rate. One man lives near a new shopping centre with cut price stores and a wide range of goods; the schools, clinics, and libraries may be modern and well-equipped and there may be plenty of employment opportunities for his wife and children. The other man's family may have none of these things, unless they make a long and expensive journey. Now these differences between different parts of the country or different parts of a city are well known and may be documented from a variety of statistical sources. The point may be simply made by picking a small random sample of addresses in any area and working out how much it would cost, and how long it would take, for an inhabitant in these houses to get an urgent doctor's prescription, if they were all given the prescription at the same time. However, although the point may be obvious it is rarely systematically discussed as an important and fundamental constraint on life chances. In this respect spatial structure influences social structure.

Social and political intervention

All states intervene to redress the unequal distribution of power in relation to important resources such as housing and urban facilities. The nature and type of intervention will vary according to the specific ideologies and historical experience of the society concerned. The motives for this intervention may range from an altruistic concern for the situation of one's fellow men to the fear that unless something is given all may be taken by force. The concern for higher standards in housing has forced up the cost of economic rents, hence those who do the less-well-paid jobs find it difficult, if not impossible, to provide shelter for themselves. The government and local authorities, therefore, have to subsidise the poor in order to maintain the standards they themselves have set. To take a further example, green belts are established round the major urban areas such as London or Birmingham. These are often described as 'lungs' for the city, where people can drive out for picnics, play golf or go bird-watching. Certainly it is 'better' for some people that they should be able to pursue these activities at less cost to themselves. However, other people, who work in the city, but who for various reasons are unable to buy a house within the area surrounded by the green belt, are obliged to pay extra journey-to-work costs in order to cross the green belt, between home and work. By limiting the size of settlements or by attempting to control the location of industry, planning affects the life chances of those living in specific localities.

Urban and regional planning, together with other instruments of social policy, play a crucial role in a mixed economy in redistributing spatial resources. In some cases the power position of a minority may be reinforced by planning decisions, as when the trading and commercial interests in a town are reinforced in their dominant position. Those with property are more directly affected by land-use planning than those without. Since property owners are quick to defend their own interests, planners are more likely to be aware of the impact their decisions will have on them. They may be less aware of the implications for those without property, who are often less articulate.

The socio-ecological system

In the same way that industrial sociologists consider techniques, technology and a socio-technical system in their studies of industrialism and industrial man, so, too, must the urban sociologist consider the way this socio-technical system operates spatially in the study of urbanism and urban man. However, few sociologists feel that the adjective 'urban' is necessary in urbanised societies such as Britain or the United States. Industrial sociologists may feel that factory gates shut out enough of the rest of society to justify a distinctive specialism, whereas 'urban' is everywhere. However, the type of urban environment does seem to be an important variable and some industrial sociologists are now arguing that it is not possible to separate the work situation from the social and spatial environment in which it is encapsulated. Goldthorpe (1966) has argued, in a recent article on car assembly workers that these workers define work 'as an essentially instrumental activity—as a means to ends external to the work situation'. In order to understand the nature of the work orientation of these men, the non-work aspects of their lives, such as their 'experience of both social and geographical mobility, their position in the life-cycle and their present patterns of family and community living' need to be investigated. The problem is to evolve a conceptual framework into which this kind of information can be fitted for distinctive subgroups in society. The emergence of distinctive styles of life as ends in themselves, related to the work situation, but not entirely determined by it, is a characteristic feature of urban society. The fundamental constraints and restrictions may now be more severely imposed by the socio-ecological system—housing, distribution of employment, journey to work and so on—than by the work situation alone.

The economic substructure creates authority/compliance relationships and differential rewards in terms of power, wealth and prestige. Much of the pattern thus created is related to the techniques and technology involved in a given work situation. Yet men do not move out of the socio-technical system when they leave the factory gates. It is the non-work aspects of socio-technical system which I have called the socio-ecological system.

We may conclude this section by raising an important question. Is there an inherent logic in the organisation of urban space in advanced industrial societies, dependent on the level of technology, towards which all societies are inevitably drawn, no matter what the political system or pattern of economic activity? There is an obvious difference between societies in the amount of publicly built housing—whether by the state or by any other public authority. Yet such a difference by itself, is not very revealing: much depends on whether the public authority works within a capitalist system and has to purchase land for its own needs on the open market. In this case those who, by virtue of their relationship to the housing market, are dependent on public housing may be at a disadvantage compared with those in a society where public authorities are not so limited in their ability to acquire suitable land. Again, the government policy towards public housing may in some societies fluctuate considerably over a relatively short period, so that at one period some sections of society are favoured and at another time a different section is favoured. Such fluctuations will be reflected in the urban form, and certain sections of the population, which may have been favoured in the past, may retain their advantage even when policies and parties change. This point is clearly illustrated in Musil's study of Prague (in Pahl ed., 1968) where changes in government policy had a direct impact on the urban social structure.

In conclusion, the built environment is a result of conflicts, taking place in the past and in the present, between those with different degrees of power in society—landowners, planners, developers, estate agents, local authorities, pressure groups of all kinds, insurance companies and so on. As the balance of power between these elements changes and as ideologies in society rise and fall, so the built environment is affected. It is a continuing situation, with the past constraining the present and together binding and limiting the future. As conflict over differential access to essential ingredients of socially defined styles of life increases, space and housing as important, yet scarce resources, will need to be incorporated more effectively into sociological analysis. For an example of this we may now look in some detail at a particular study of conflict over housing.

COMPETITION AND CONFLICT OVER HOUSING

In their study of race relations in the Sparkbrook district of Birmingham Professor John Rex and Robert Moore of the University of Durham based part of their analysis on the concept of housing classes. This section is directly based on their work.

The emergence of subcultural styles

Three main elements become segregated from each other during the early growth of the city. First, the upper-middle class or 'captains of industry' lived in substantial family houses. Economically and socially independent, and secure in their possession of capital and property, they were able to develop their own distinctive style of community living relatively close to the centre of the city. Katharine Chorley has described this upper-middle-class style of life in her autobiographical account *Manchester Made Them* and is well worth reading in this context. Secondly, those who were employed by the upper-middle class, as so many rent-paying hands, were housed in rows of little cottages, and for them common deprivation helped to create common solidarity. A common culture emerged in which extrafamilial kin, pubs and chapels, the trade unions and the friendly societies were of great importance. 'Mutual aid rather than property gave security to the inhabitants and when that mutual aid was expressed in political terms in the socialism of the city hall it was greatly to enhance the power of the established working classes in their struggle for housing and living space': Richard Hoggart's *The Uses of Literacy* describe this culture acutely and sympathetically.

The final category, which began to emerge towards the end of the nineteenth century, was socially and economically between the two main categories; this category shopkeepers, clerks and other lower-middle class people, aspired to the style of life of the upper-middle class and went as close towards it as their more limited means would allow. Such people are brilliantly caricatured in *The Diary of a Nobody* by G. and W. Grossmith which was first published in 1892.

Such is a somewhat oversimplified model of the social structure which produced the spatial structure of the city of Birmingham seventy years ago. It is based on the industrial and employment structure of the time and reflects contemporary ideologies and the distribution of power. This structure then became fossilised in bricks and mortar so that the houses still stand in what is now an inner zone but which, when the houses were built, was the edge of the city.

The urban game of leapfrog

With time the large family houses cease to be so convenient or so fashionable. The increase in population, the development of the motor car, buses and trams all served to push the upper-middle class to large detached houses, gaining quietness and privacy and large secluded gardens, further out from the city centre. The lower-middle class may have had to leap further out to their semidetached houses, with gardens back and front, and were dependent on the availablity of cheap land and their ability to borrow capital. The working class were also able to join in this suburban game by using the power they had gained in local government to build cheaper replicas of white-collar housing, also on the cheaper land at the periphery. Thus a new public suburbia paralleled the private suburbia. The demand for cheap land and space, coupled with the inevitable decay of older properties creates a pattern of central decline and peripheral expansion, which continues until the core is renewed.

The urban socio-cultural system

The leapfrogging suburban development implies a general acceptance of the middle-class style of life as a common aspiration for all sections of the population. It is because of these common values and common objectives that there is conflict over housing. Those who are left behind in the centre of the city may still accept the urban value system, which implies that they are at the back of a queue to move to the most desired style of life in the suburbs. Hence, those who live in the city's inner ring are more likely to see their stay there as *transitional*. Rex and Moore (1967) see this urban central status-value system as crucial in understanding the problems of this zone of transition: 'Any attempt to segregate the inhabitants of this area permanently is bound to involve conflict. The long-term destiny of a city which frustrates the desire to improve their status by segregationalist policies is some sort of urban riot' (p. 9).

Housing classes

Thus housing, and particularly certain kinds of desirable suburban housing, is a scarce resource and people are differentially placed in the basic competition or conflict for it. Shelter may be obtained in three main ways: whole houses may be made available to those who have access to credit or capital; houses may be allocated by local authorities according to certain formal bureaucratic criteria such as length of residence, size of family, health and so on; finally, there is the free market in housing space. Hence there is competition for the use of sites and also competition for the use of buildings, long since abandoned by their original owners. Rex and Moore (1967) see this class struggle over the use of houses as the central process of the city as a social unit. Men in the same position in the job market may still have differential degrees of access to housing, depending on such factors as their length of residence, colour of skin pigmentation, access to capital, number of dependents and so on. The following are the housing classes distinguished by Rex and Moore:

(*a*) The outright owners of large houses in desirable areas.
(*b*) Mortgage payers who 'own' whole houses in desirable areas.
(*c*) Council tenants in council-built houses.
(*d*) Council tenants in slum houses awaiting demolition.
(*e*) Tenants of a whole house owned by a private landlord.
(*f*) Owners of a house bought with short-term loans who are compelled to let rooms in order to meet their repayment obligations.
(*g*) Tenants of rooms in a lodging house.

These housing classes are arranged in a hierarchy of prestige or status and will follow a definite territorial distribution in the city, dependent on the age and size of the buildings. There is likely to be a movement over time from classes (g), (f), (e), and (d) aspiring to (c) or, possibly, for those who may get access to capital, to (b). To the extent that this movement does, in fact, take place and the less privileged feel that such movement is likely for them and also feel that the position of the privileged is legitimate, then it would be more accurate to describe the situation as a status system. Where there is a basic conflict or struggle over housing then the term 'housing class' may be used. Rex and Moore (1967) claim that 'being a member of one or other of these classes is of first importance in determining a man's associations, his interest, his life style and his position in the urban social structure' (p. 36).

Housing classes in the zone of transition

Inevitably newcomers without large amounts of capital must seek shelter in the zone of transition, that is the converted middle-class houses of the inner rings of the city. The immigrant who borrows from relatives and friends, may, with the help of the bank or money-lender, acquire sufficient capital on a short-term basis for him to buy a lodging house and repay the loan if he gets a high enough income from rents. Thus, there is a need for houses in which no one else has a long-term interest, with sufficient rooms to ensure a high rent income. Those who rent the rooms will be those who value the anonymity and impersonal market relationship with the landlord, and those who simply cannot find alternative accommodation. Hence such districts will include immigrants, 'deviants' of one sort and another, people with irregular forms of family life, and so on. Characterised by overcrowding, high rents, lack of privacy and no choice in neighbours, such a housing situation produces a very diverse housing class which 'lacks the capacity and perhaps the desire to organise itself as an interest group. The discharged prisoner, the deserted wife, the coloured immigrant and the prostitute have little in common except their housing conditions' (Rex and Moore 1967, p. 38). This section of the population has to be housed and 'A pariah group of landlords is needed who will do an essential job and take the blame for doing it' (pp. 40–1).

The landlord is not in a strong position. He may have been ob-liged to pay a very high deposit—perhaps up to 50 per cent of the cost of the house—and he is obliged to repay the rent at a high rate of interest, perhaps 8 per cent. Indeed, he may be repaying both a bank and building society and his friends or relatives at the same time. The houses will produce very little capital when sold: those built in the 1880s and 1890s probably have 99 year leases which ex-pire in ten or fifteen years' time. Inevitably, multi-occupation leads to neglect, as tenants have no stake in maintaining the value of the property. Furthermore, Pakistani landlords may feel obliged to pro-vide accommodation for their kinsmen either rent-free or at a nominal charge of £1 a week. This cuts his total income, since there is a limit which he can hope to squeeze from his other tenants. These may include more than his fair share of deviants or those with large families, who give the fabric of the property hard use. Thus the debt-burdened landlord, surrounded by difficult tenants, is unlikely to have much money with which to maintain, far less improve, the property.

The very tight constraints, which limit the private landlord in the zone of transition, are shown even more acutely in the Milner Holland Report on *Housing in Greater London* (Cmd. 2605, 1965). London, with less than a fifth of the total stock of dwellings, had well over half of all the multi-occupied dwellings in the country and it is appropriate to conclude this section by quoting directly from the report:

The cost of house purchase and upkeep is therefore *forcing* people, in their desire to be owner-occupiers, 'to indulge in the worst type of sub-letting and multiple occupation' . . . (p. 80).
Our conclusion from this survey was that a family on an average or below average income would have been *forced* to live in two rooms at the most or even one . . . (p. 94).
The families that *lose the race* for scarce accommodation are by no means all 'problem' families; the most common is the unskilled worker with wife and several children, and in many cases their below average income has been reduced by unemployment or sickness (p. 94) (my italics).

CONSTRAINT AND CHOICE IN A COMMUTER VILLAGE

There is a danger that the notion of housing classes will become associated solely with the decaying zone of transition in the twilight areas of our large urban concentrations. Hence, in this final section, we will consider the housing situation in a commuter village in the outer metropolitan area of south-east England. These different categories are not necessarily represented in any one village but are the constituent social elements in this particular physical context. The different housing situations may be listed as follows:

1. *Large property owners*

Those who own large acreages or who have considerable capital resources live in the largest mansions, ranging from 'stately homes' to 'charming Queen Anne farmhouses'. In some villages the large landowner may be the only ratepayer and he may own adjoining parishes as well. His property is a constraint by his sentimental family links.

2. *Salaried immigrants with some capital*

Those who aspire to a certain style of life associated with a 'heritage house' require modest capital resources, since it is less likely that building societies will grant substantial loans for older property which requires expensive maintenance. For such people the type of house is more important than the particular place, although space and seclusion may be as much characteristic of the place as the house. Those who do not inherit capital but get high salaries may save the £15–£20,000 to buy a 'period' property by their forties and may be able to make others think that their wealth is more deeply rooted.

3. *Spiralists*

Those employees in large-scale organisations who are obliged to change their place of residence as they move through and up the status hierarchies of these organisations have been called 'cosmopolitans', 'non-traditionalists' or 'spiralists' by sociologists. Local government officers, managers in industry, and even teachers, whose careers follow this pattern, may feel that they can integrate themselves more readily into a small-scale community. Such people are often seeking a particular place rather than a particular house or plot, and without capital would be obliged to buy a modern house on a mortgage.

4. *Those with limited income and little capital*

These are the reluctant commuters who simply want a new house at a price they can afford. The price of land is kept high in the towns by the planners, who release only limited quantities which fit the calculations they have made of housing needs up to ten or fifteen years ahead. However, the London housing market extends widely into the outer metropolitan area and marginal home owners may be obliged to travel further in order to get a slightly cheaper house. At this level a few hundred pounds may make a big difference: the intervention of planning between the job market and the housing market is crucial for this category.

5. *The retired*

This is a very mixed category; some come for the environmental qualities of the area, others because bungalows are cheaper than in the towns. All are very likely to be very dependent on transport to get them to facilities and for very old people this may present acute problems.

6. *Council house tenants*

The accident of birth is the strongest criterion for the allocation of a local authority house in a village. Most tenants are obliged to leave the villages to find employment. They are simply manual workers living in a small estate surrounded by fields because they were either born there or have lived there long enough to qualify.

7. *Tied cottagers and other tenants*

Those who work in the agricultural industry may find that their employer is also their landlord. This may be a considerable constraint: with low wages they may be unable to improve their house and the farmer may be unwilling or unable to spend money on improvements. Some old people may also live in houses, which are rent free, or at a peppercorn rent, but rarely will the physical conditions be very satisfactory in such circumstances.

8. *Local tradesmen and owners of small businesses*

These people are part of the minority with a strong economic interest in the area. They are less likely to feel constrained, since they can generally afford a house appropriate to their status.

These eight categories illustrate the diversity of the social situation in a metropolitan village of perhaps a thousand inhabitants. Category 1 is tied to the locality by property, although that does not necessarily mean that they are obliged to take up residence. Categories 2 and 3 have been able to choose either the house or locality which suits their style of life because of the power their capital or income gives them. Most of those in categories 4 and 6 are forced out from the village by the job market, though the housing market forces them to live there. In category 7 both job and house limit some to the locality. Thus there are degrees of choice and degrees of constraint. Paradoxically, there is no village population as such; rather there are specific populations which for various, but identifiable, reasons find themselves in a village.

Both the zone of transition in a great metropolis and a small commuter village in a metropolitan region illustrate in their distinctive ways the relationship between housing situations and a socio-ecological system.

THE CASE STUDIES AND THEIR LIMITATIONS

During the last twenty years sociologists have described the pattern of social life in a variety of urban contexts in Britain. Working-class areas of cities have attracted the greatest interest and there are useful accounts of estates in Sheffield, Liverpool, Coventry and of inner parts of cities such as Bethnal Green in London, St Ebbes in Oxford, and 'Crown Street' in Liverpool. Descriptive studies of middle-class areas are less common, although studies emphasising family relationships have been carried out in two middle-class areas of London (Highgate and Woodford) and in some provincial towns such as Banbury and Swansea. There are certain difficulties and problems in using these studies as a basis for generalisation about patterns of social life and before considering some of this case-study material in detail certain limitations need to be mentioned.

Limitations of time

One of the best-known studies of working-class life in urban areas is *Family and Kinship in East London* by Michael Young and Peter Willmott. For many people this is taken to be the standard account of how a certain section of the British population lives today. However, the research was carried out between 1953 and 1955. Television was hardly part of the culture then; few working-class people had motor cars, and consumer goods such as washing machines and refrigerators were much rarer in working-class homes than they are now. Of course, this limitation must not be overstated: the impact of consumer durables on style of life is not as revolutionary as, for example, advertisements would have us believe. However, television has kept many men at home when they might have gone out to the pub or club, with consequent implications for family life. And the increasing ownership of private motor cars will enable an increasing proportion of the working class to keep in touch with extra-familial kin who live some distance away.

Limitations of place

Careful statistical studies of census information, and particularly the study of *British Towns* by C. A. Moser and Wolf Scott, have demonstrated the great social and economic diversity of British towns. On almost every variable, for which information is available, there is a large and striking range between towns. If, for example, we take an index of health—say mortality from bronchitis—and compare local standardised rates, with the national rate taken as 100, then, in 1951 Esher had a rate of 23 and Salford had a rate of 277. Similarly, taking the percentage of the occupied population aged twenty to twenty-four in 1951, whose terminal education age was less than fifteen, Beckenham had 33·6 per cent and Stoke had 86·2 per cent. The Moser and Scott study showed that some 125 out of 157 towns appeared among the extremes in one table or another.

Since it has to be demonstrated that the diversity of British towns is getting any less, then one must be careful not to assume that a study of Banbury or Swansea necessarily provides a microcosm of our society. Of course social processes are more likely to have general validity than social patterns and this is a theme to which we shall return later.

Limitations of objectives

Different studies by different research workers using different techniques and concerned with different problems will produce different results. This may appear a blinding glimpse of the obvious yet very often the point is not remembered. The authors of the twenty or thirty case studies generally did not use the same definitions for sub-categories of their population, nor did they systematically gather a minimum amount of comparable data. For example, the study of social conditions in central Liverpool in 1955–56 published as *Urban Redevelopment and Social Change* by Vereker, Mays *et al.* (1961) was motivated by a concern with community problems, with the intention of making a contribution to social planning. Special attention was given to the residents' reactions to change in an attempt to find out how much they wanted to remain in central Liverpool or move out to new estates on the periphery. Hence the study is mainly descriptive, a snapshot of contemporary history, objectively presented for planners and administrators. Such social description or sociography is extremely valuable for local decisionmakers and the market research type of study, relating to choices between perceived alternatives, will always be very important. However, if there are no specifically *sociological* questions posed at the outset of the study then it is less likely that the study will help to deepen understanding of social relationships or society in general. The main conclusions of the Liverpool study were that some kind of balance should be achieved between the disruptive effects of urban renewal on established patterns of social relationships and the obligation to provide better physical conditions for those 'who wish to improve their social status and to begin a new life in a totally different locality'. By addressing themselves primarily to planners the authors of the Liverpool study imposed limitations on themselves and on their potential contribution to sociology. Does a new home, and possibly greater affluence, *necessarily* produce a changed conception of society with new aspirations for patterns of behaviour? This is an issue which has concerned sociologists over the past decade but on which the Liverpool study provides no clue.

If the Liverpool study is compared with the Swansea study *The Family and Social Change* by Colin Rosser and Christopher Harris (1965), the contrast is acute. At Swansea an effort is made to relate the work to previous studies so that not only does it help to deepen our understanding of the family in urban society but also emphasises the diversity of locality social systems and the distinctiveness of the Swansea situation. As the title suggests, the emphasis is on kinship and, appropriately, one of the authors is an anthropologist. However, family relationships are related to changes in the industrial structure of Swansea in such a way that the conclusions can be generalised to industrial society as a whole.

The stereotyping of class

The contrast between middle-class life styles and traditional working-class life styles is often so great within or between localities that such differences are emphasised to the neglect of more subtle and sometimes more important distinctions. We know more about working class patterns of social behaviour in the traditional and, very often declining, industries such as coal-mining, and much less about, say, workers in the building or transport and communication industries. Similarly, we know something about the established middle class of Woodford or Banbury but next to nothing of the upper middle class of Central London or of the south-east commuter land.

THE PRINCIPAL DETERMINANTS OF URBAN WAYS OF LIFE

We have seen that the various descriptive studies of patterns of family and other social life vary widely in quality and intent. Planners and other practical men may be forgiven if they express irritation at the lack of any systematic presentation of sociologists' insights. There are, however, certain fundamental variables generally implicit in most community studies. We will discuss some of the most important of these variables, or constraints, in turn.

Stage in the family cycle

Some research workers, such as Dr Mark Abrams, who have examined the way in which the population as a whole spend their time and money, have concluded that stage in the family cycle is a more significant variable than social class. The assumption is that, say, men over the age of sixty-five have more in common because of that, than the fact that they were previously working in middle or working-class occupations. Dr Abrams has calculated for the year 1962 that 46 million out of a total population of 52 million could be allocated to one of eight stages, as Table 5 illustrates.

TABLE 5
Stages in the family cycle

Stage	Age group	% of total population	Approximate numbers (millions)
1. Infants and school children	0–14	26	12·0
2. Young unmarried	15–24	12	5·5
3. Young married, no children	15–34	3	1·5
4. Young marrieds with children	15–34	12	5·5
5. Middle married, with children	35–44	11	5·0
6. Older married, children	45–64	5	2·3
7. Older married, no children at home	45–64	18	8·2
8. Pension	65 and over	13	6·0
		100	46·0

Source: Mark Abrams, *Communities and Social Change*, National Council of Social Service, 1964.

Now it is clear enough that people at the same stage in the family cycle will have certain needs in common. This does not, of course, mean that they have equal access to the facilities to meet these needs. We have already seen that characteristics such as occupation or number of years spent in full time education are not randomly spread about urban areas but that people with such characteristics are segregated to a greater or lesser degree. Hence physical distance between homes and desired facilities such as shops, clinics, schools, libraries, and so on will vary considerably. Of course this distance may be less of a constraint on the young unmarrieds than to those over sixty-five. However, whatever the age groups, some means of overcoming this distance by private or public transport is crucial. The wife of a semiskilled manual worker living on a new council estate, recently built on the cheaper land at the edge of the built-up area, and entirely dependent on an expensive and infrequent bus service to the town centre, is in quite a different situation from a middle-class woman of the same age and stage in her family-building cycle, who can drive herself about in her own car. The point can be made in a more extreme form by comparing the pensioner, who can only afford to walk, with his affluent contemporary using a chauffeur or taxi.

Finally, even though people at the same stage in their family cycle may have certain objective needs in common, they may not perceive that they have these needs. A study of child-rearing practices in Nottingham, for example, revealed that middle-class mothers were more informed than working class mothers about the maternity benefits and services available to them and were more ready to ask or to insist that they should receive them (J. and E. Newson, 1963).

Connectedness of social network

A number of studies have demonstrated a connection between the pattern of relationships external to the conjugal or nuclear family and the pattern of relationships within it. Any given conjugal pair will have a number of friends, neighbours and relatives who may or may not know each other. The degree to which these people all know one another can be described, by analogy, in terms of a network. The closeness of the mesh of the net depends on how many of those in a given individual's social world know one another and the thickness of the strands would depend on how well such people know each other. Empirical studies have documented the close-knit social networks of long-established and traditional working-class areas and have noted the relationship between this social pattern and the husband-wife relationship, which tends to be more sharply segregated: women deal with the home and children, and gossip with relatives, men have their separate world of work, friends and pub or club. Where a conjugal couple live in a loose-knit network husbands and wives are more likely to share household tasks and also to share in joint social activities.

It would be wrong to assume that loose-knit networks are an essentially middle-class characteristic or that tight-knit networks are characteristically working-class, although there is some likelihood of this connection. A crucial determinant is the degree of geographical mobility which the household has had. Where an individual was born, went to school, worked, married and settled down in the same area, obviously the likelihood of such a person's friends and relatives knowing each other are high. Typically such an unchanging pattern emerges in a long settled area with a stable or slowly expanding economy and with a good balance of local employment to the local age structure. With unstable employment opportunities there is likely to be a higher turnover of population and a proportion of school leavers may be obliged to leave home for work elsewhere. It is less likely for such a stable pattern to emerge for the middle class, who typically expect their offspring to leave home for higher education or employment and ultimately to settle elsewhere. However, in provincial England there is a traditional middle class which centres round commerce and the professions at a local level. Most local grammar schools produce a small local elite who settle in the area, marry amongst themselves and continue a social life within a fairly tight-knit network. There is a degree of segregation, in that the men meet at the Old Boys' Club, sports clubs, the premises of the local branch of their political party, the Rotary Club and so on. The women run the local charities, the Townswomen's Guild, various church or chapel activities, and so on. These middle-class 'burgesses', as they have been called, may also have segregated conjugal roles.

A close-knit network is an important means of social control and hence the pattern of middle-class life in provincial England is reinforced and the traditional working-class communities in the cities perpetuate themselves. For the working class the close-knit network encapsulates them, cutting them off from the wider society; for the middle class the connectedness of the network is far more a pattern of choice reflecting a valued style of life.

The occupational and industrial structure of the town or city

We have already seen that differences in class consciousness between Oldham, Shields and Northampton in the nineteenth century can be related to the distinctive occupational and industrial structures of these towns. The same disparity exists today between the large, solidaristic and strike-prone concentrations of miners, dockers or ship-building workers and the deferential, Conservative-voting, working class of the cathedral cities, with little industrial employment and low wage rates. Again, considering the proportion of women in the labour force, although the national average is about one-third, there is a range between such places as Gosport, Scunthorpe or Gillingham where only about one-fifth of the women are employed to the textile towns of Rochdale, Burnley and Blackburn where some two-fifths of the women are in the labour force.

Perhaps the principal determinants of traditional working-class culture are poverty and insecurity. Kinship ties are to the traditional working class what property is to the traditional middle class: an important source of economic security and support. Thus in areas of industrial decline—such as the old coal-mining areas of the northeast—a policy of encouraging labour mobility may be frustrated by the reluctance of the workers to sever or stretch kinship links, which themselves are being strengthened by the insecurity produced by the economic uncertainty. Hence there is a vicious circle: the process which produces the need for labour mobility is the same process which engenders the defensive mechanism of kinship solidarity, which impedes mobility.

Equally important is the development of occupational communities in one-industry, one-class towns or in areas where there is sufficient variety of manual employment so that social and geographical mobility is low. Here work-mates are leisure-time companions and a communal sociability becomes almost ritualistic, reinforcing the sense of belonging to a work-dominated collectivity.

However, workers in service occupations, in small-scale enterprises and with more autonomy in their work may have a more private, home-centred existence. Often housed on new council or cheap privately built estates, with few recreational amenities and lacking the social skills to create new styles of sociability, status is attributed by what a person has, rather than what he is, as revealed by long-standing interaction.

Among the middle class the variation may be equally great and differences in life style may relate to type of occupation and scale of organisation. Research by Professor Wilensky in the United States has shown that the difference in amount of leisure time between, say, lawyers working for themselves, as opposed to lawyers working for a company is marked, the difference within this category being greater than the difference in leisure time between all professionals and low manual workers. Similarly, Wilensky (1960, 1961) has shown that those with more orderly careers—that is, moving fairly systematically up the steps of a bureaucratic hierarchy—are more likely to participate more frequently in community associations than those whose careers show a more disorderly shift between jobs. He argues that occupation, career pattern, mobility orientation and work milieu, with the associated educational experiences, are becoming increasingly more crucial variables for determining style of life than social class alone.

These differences *within* the broad categories of middle and working class are becoming of much greater interest to sociologists and are discussed in companion volumes in this series. The important point to stress in the present context is the direct relationship between the local industrial and occupational structure, with the associated pattern of growth and decline, and the style of life of local population categories.

RECENT ATTEMPTS AT SYNTHESIS

It would be difficult and unnecessary to summarise the two recent works of synthesis: this would be to move too far from the original empirical studies. However, it is valuable to consider the basis of the synthesis in each case. Josephine Klein is a social psychologist and her emphasis is on small group behaviour and in particular the relationship between subcultural styles and early patterns of socialisation. Ronald Frankenberg also attempts synthesis of community studies, ranging them along what he calls a 'morphological continuum', related to economic diversification and increase in scale. Both these authors draw on much of the same case material but worked independently of each other. It is interesting and instructive to compare the different frameworks and the different levels of emphasis of these studies, if only to induce a critical attitude in students coming to the case studies or their synthesisers for the first time. Clearly one does not know all about rural or urban Britain after reading three or four monographs and even if one is familiar with most or all of these locality studies, there are still differences of interpretation which need to be carefully evaluated.

Samples from English cultures

Dr Klein (1965) produced a long book, running to nearly 700 pages, in two volumes. The first section is devoted to extensive summaries of culturally isolated working-class life reported by other research workers in an area of Paddington in the late 1940s, 'Ship Street' in Liverpool in the early 1950s and the Yorkshire mining village of 'Ashton', also in the early 1950s. Essentially, Dr Klein's argument is that we are what other people let us be.

[A man's] personality, in terms of which he now experiences the world, has itself been formed by what happened to him in the past, and so on, regressively, back to childhood, infancy and the womb. Experiences in early life have to be regarded as especially significant because they impinge on a more fluid, less rigidly formed personality structure. To round off the circle of argument, the personalities of most adults will, by virtue of their parental role, provide a part—at first an overwhelmingly important part— of the experiences of the next generation (Klein, 1965, p. xi).

This emphasis on early childhood experience occurs throughout the book, although it is the third and final section which is primarily devoted to childrearing practices. However, socialisation is emphasised in the first section where the vicious circle of cultural deprivation is clearly presented: economic insecurity is coupled with emotional insecurity; there is little incentive to apply foresight or effort to secure anything; the environment is experienced as unpredictable and hostile. For example, children in the zone of transition at Paddington are promised treats to keep them quiet but these never materialise; when told they are going to the seaside they may end up being taken to hospital by their mother, who simply lies to them without thinking. A combination of a whole host of individually minor and almost trivial activities in the relationship of parents to children helps to perpetuate a particular character type in a particular area. Dr Klein is interested in the *mechanisms* which create the sub-cultural styles. She is less interested in the economic and physical context. One might add in passing that there is very little suggestion that housing and environmental conditions contribute in any fundamental way to the social pattern of cultural deprivation described by the authors she quotes.

In the second section of her work Dr Klein is concerned with aspects of adult life in England—how the majority of English people live. First, traditional working-class life is described, focused, inevitably, round a discussion of family life—social networks and conjugal relationships, the central role of 'mum', adolescence and courtship, parents' relationships with their children and so on. Working-class life is family life: the family is the working-class equivalent of property. Then follows a chapter concerned with changes in working-class life, with particular reference to life on municipal housing estates, and this is an extremely valuable synthesis of the material which students are strongly urged to read for themselves.

It is in her discussion of change that Dr Klein to some extent undermines her arguments about cultural determinism and the overwhelming importance of early patterns of socialisation, which appear in the other sections of the book. Somewhat over-forcefully Dr Klein asserts: 'All geographical changes are accompanied by social and psychological changes' (p. 232), but she also remarks, more cautiously, 'Housing estates are not to be thought of as the only places where changes take place. Rather, the argument will be that the break with tradition which a geographical move entails allows other social forces to make a relatively more forcible impact' (p. 220).

Traditional working-class life was family and community-centred, with limited occupational choice, segregated relationships between husband and wife, with fixed and traditional values and poverty always present to a greater or lesser degree. However, on the new estates social networks are inevitably more loose-knit, there is greater emphasis on the home and children, aspirations and attitudes are more individual and there is a greater concern with social mobility and achievement values. There is also a change from status assent to status dissent and it is worth considering this change in some detail.

Zweig, in his book on *The Worker in the Affluent Society* makes the following distinctions:

The working class may be divided into three groups, numerically not very far apart. One group tries to acquire property; the second does not think about house property at all as it is beyond its possibilities and its ken; the third group rejects the acquisition of house property as downright undesirable and even pernicious for the working man. People in this last group would often say: 'A house of your own is like a millstone round your neck,' or 'I wouldn't touch it, it's only worry,' or 'They want to catch you' (quoted in Klein, 1965, p. 238–9).

The first category would, therefore, be status-dissenting; the other categories are status-assenting. This is how Mogey described the status-assenters in his Oxford study:

They are less vocal; they accept the habits, standards, word usages and values typical of their area and street; they talk little about problems of class conflict, about trade unions, work or any other general topic. They are interested in specific people, in the details of daily living, and they make no general observations other than clichés or headlines from recent papers. They are not worried about the future, they make few plans for their children (quoted in Klein, 1965, p. 240).

The problem which neither Dr Klein nor the authors she quotes are able to answer is *why* some status-dissenters become status-dissenters. Why do some buy houses and other consumer goods? Why do some join voluntary associations, feel more responsible for themselves, make demands on local authorities and have ambitions for their children? There is more description than explanation of this issue. Have status-assenters been socialised differently in early childhood? Have their mothers suffered downward social mobility and become concerned to push their offspring back? Does greater affluence *in itself* produce changing family patterns and status-dissent? What causes people to reject old reference groups in favour of new ones? Some of these issues are discussed in W. G. Runciman's book *Relative Deprivation and Social Justice* and also in the series of studies on *The Affluent Worker* by Goldthorpe, *et al.* (1968–.) Clearly Dr Klein is right in emphasising patterns of childrearing and personality development but her approach has a greater explanatory power in dealing with established rather than changing situations.

Communities in Britain

Professor Frankenberg's (1966) book is quite differently arranged, although he deals with essentially the same case study material. He is concerned with *localities* rather than cultures and two-thirds of the book is made up of descriptions and summaries of locality-based studies moving from what he calls 'truly rural' through small country towns and 'communities in conurbations' to urban housing estates. These studies fall along a 'morphological continuum': 'It is morphological because although each stage is structurally more complicated than the one before, and each has a more diversified economy and technology' there is no implication that any one of them will necessarily become more alike the next one on the continuum. Nevertheless, Professor Frankenberg does see a clear direction of change and he attempts to illuminate such a change by using such concepts as role, network and class: 'While the workers live in small settlements and work in small workshops a multiplicity of ties strengthens the solidarity of regional or local groups. The growth of giant factories and urban centres rescues the workers from the 'idiocy of rural life' (pp. 258–9).

Such an assertion appears very hard to substantiate empirically. Not only does there appear to be greater class-consciousness and sharper class-conflict in the remote Cheviot parish of *Westrigg* studied by James Littlejohn (1964) but also status-assenters appear to be highly typical of the large urban centres. Professor Frankenberg asserts rather than explains by convincing argument but at least he makes his values explicit: 'I would rather enough cubic feet of housing space and an efficient milkman than three acres of land and a cow.' He would prefer a situation where the worker is alienated and estranged rather than integrated because this will make revolution more likely.

This attempt to view British community studies as a Marxian social anthropologist is very interesting and provides a lively contrast to the approach of Dr Klein. Since Dr Frankenberg honestly states his values, students have no excuse not to be alerted and should be stimulated to read some locality studies for themselves.

Ways of life and ways of interpretation

This chapter may have appeared rather negative. We have looked at both the limitations of the case studies and the limitations of those who have attempted to synthesise them. In many ways this critical stance is more important for students to acquire than simply a heap of empirical information about a given locality. The processes of change should be the essential focus of interest for the sociologist, but unfortunately our descriptive tools are better than our explanatory concepts. Description may imply understanding but not necessarily explanation. If we can explain then we can predict.

Thus it is important that this chapter is read in conjunction with one of the locality studies, describing ways of life in Britain. Perhaps the best one to start with would be Margaret Stacey's *Tradition and Change, A Study of Banbury* (1960). Students should be very critical of the processes of change: what do words such as 'urbanisation', 'bureaucratisation', 'industrialisation' and so on really mean? What quantitative changes lead to which qualitative changes in patterns of social relationships? Why are certain categories of people behaving differently in Banbury as a result of what changes? Why are certain activities, such as voluntary associations, described in considerable detail, whereas others, such as social relationships in factories and workshops, receive scarcely a mention? What sort of book might Professor Frankenberg have written about Banbury if he had been working there at the same time? How would this differ from the sort of book Dr Klein might have written? However, it is of great interest that a restudy of Banbury is being currently undertaken and one may look forward to a book in a few years' time, which will enable Mrs Stacey and colleagues to re-evaluate the earlier study in the light of developments in the town and developments in techniques of sociological analysis, which have emerged during the intervening years.

Formal voluntary associations 6

By and large for the working class community life is no different
from family life, whereas for the middle class community life very
often implies joining voluntary associations. People join in activities
with others, apart from friends and kin, either because they want to
express themselves by playing, acting, listening, drinking or whatever, or because they want to achieve certain specific ends such as
defend themselves, negotiate for higher wages, prevent some activity
defined as undesirable from taking place and so on. Such associations
are *secondary* as opposed to the *primary* group of friends, neighbours
and kin. These secondary associations may be either *expressive* or
instrumental as we have seen. They may be interpreted as a reflection
of the degree of collectively-mindedness of a locality and may serve
as a valuable guide to the local social structure and local behaviour.
They have the added advantage of being relatively easy to investigate
and sociologists have taken advantage of this convenience by studying
them in some detail, thus furthering our understanding of social processes in general.

A number of surveys of club membership and attendance have
documented the fact that such organisations attract middle-class
people more than the working class. In their study of the London
suburb of Woodford, Willmott and Young showed that nearly twice
as many middle-class as working-class people had attended at least
one club in the previous month, and over a half belonged to an
organisation, compared with a third of the working-class people.
Studies in Derby (Cauter and Downham, 1954), Glossop (Birch,
1959), and 'Squirebridge' (Bottomore, 1954), document the same
trend: local formal organisations are run by and for the middle class.
'Whether [in Woodford] the avowed purpose is to play golf or
squash, to act or sing, to advance the cause of literature or Conserva-

tism, the United Nations or local trade—whatever the *overt* purpose, one result is that you meet other people' (Willmott and Young, 1960, p. 90). And the other people are all 'people-like-ourselves'—the middle class. As Margaret Stacey remarks in her analysis of voluntary associations in Banbury, 'social comfort decides which club you join and social comfort is promoted if the club is homogenous from the point of view of status'.

ASSOCIATIONAL LIFE IN THE TRADITIONAL WORKING CLASS

A common statement made at conferences, arranged to enquire into the 'lack of community spirit' or the 'apathy' of 'those unwilling to assume responsibility', is that 'it's always the same (middle-class) people who have to run everything'. Simmel, writing some sixty years ago, provides some analytical insight on this problem.

In general, and reserving many modifications, we can say that the lower a group is as a whole and the more, therefore, every member of it is accustomed to subordination, the less will the group allow one of its members to rule it. And, inversely, the higher a group is as a whole, the more likely it is that it subordinates itself only to one of its peers. In the first case, domination by the member, the like person, is difficult because everyone is low; in the second case it is easier because everybody stands high. (Simmel, Wolff, ed, 1950, p. 219).

Simmel's point may be illustrated by an interesting piece of research into the organisation of 41 Coronation street parties in Birkenhead. In this study Broady (1956) was concerned with two main questions: first, in what circumstances do people join in local social activities and, secondly, what factors influence the emergence of local leaders? This particular part of Birkenhead is known as Rock Ferry and is considered to be more respectable than the 'rougher' working-class districts which adjoin it. Social distance is maintained despite physical propinquity and a proper respect for individual and family privacy is observed. 'We're good neighbours with everybody; but you can be neighbourly without letting people over your doorstep. We keep ourselves to ourselves. There's no sitting in each other's houses like there is in some streets.' Characteristically such people are 'particular', try hard to maintain standards in spite of adversities and difficulties, and make it a matter of pride to keep themselves out of debt during periods of unemployment. A pattern of informal neighbourliness has arisen out of shared experiences and communal action may be acceptable in times of adversity. Thus, collections to help the sick or to buy a wreath are common, but communal response to a neighbour's marriage or the birth of a child is unusual. When neighbours do cooperate to meet particular contingencies this is done spontaneously and no one is considered to be primarily responsible. There were, however, certain people regarded as being specially qualified to perform particular services. One woman would have the reputation of being able to advise about children's ailments; another woman was known as 'a Labour woman' and she would act as a gatekeeper, bringing matters to the notice of the local councillor, or would help in the composition of official letters. In each of twenty-five streets, there was a person who was regularly called upon to organise bus trips, and in nine streets, one who was responsible for organising a money club. It was this tradition of informal cooperation which served as a background to the formal organisation of Coronation street parties.

The decision to start was frequently made by a small group of neighbours meeting in the street. Even those who had organised parties previously were unwilling to take it upon themselves to make the proposal. Often parents were pushed into action by their children, who knew of plans in other streets. There are good reasons why people should not be eager to take on such tasks. It would involve extra strain, tension and, of course, hard work. In particular it might involve trouble.

'Trouble' may be expected of any kind of social intercourse. Its significance is suggested by the large number of synonyms, such as 'unpleasantness', 'disagreeableness', 'itch', 'bother', 'upset', which are commonly used in its place. So expected is trouble, that it was very common to hear an organiser comment about a party with some relief that 'there wasn't a word afterwards', by which she meant that there had been no word of complaint. The organisers feared that should their neighbours feel displeased about some aspect of the organisation, they might criticise or talk adversely about them, especially behind their backs. Hence they took precautions to avoid the outbreak of trouble, 'so there will be no argument, so as not to give them a chance to talk' (Broady, 1956, p. 233).

The collection and handling of money presented problems and was particularly likely to be criticised and lead to trouble; collecting from door to door was felt to be undignified. Trouble may also be caused if the organiser failed to treat participants equally. It developed in one street when only enough bunting was brought to decorate alternate houses; in another, when the cakes, which were left over, were not shared out equally. Often the most trivial matters could cause contention. On the principle of not looking for trouble the organisers went out of their way to avoid doing anything which might give rise to later insinuations. Thus two people would collect money together, at least one woman would accompany the organiser when buying supplies or presents, and accounts were strictly kept.

The chief justification for all the organisation involved in holding these parties was that it was necessary for the children. Two-thirds of the organisers were middle-aged married women with children still at school. Of the forty-one organisers of the parties, twenty-four were 'customary organisers' some of whom had previous experience in the Co-operative Women's Guild or the Labour Party.

Both contributors and organisers disliked formality.

They frequently pointed out that theirs was not 'a proper' or 'a recognised committee'. 'Proper' committees were considered to be less friendly than their own meetings. 'Committees', it was said, 'only start little differences,' and it was thought that their members tended to become jealous of, and to find themselves at cross-purposes with one another. In the comment 'It was not just a committee, we all worked together,' the apprehensiveness of formal organisation finds a clear expression, in which a criticism of our traditional way of conducting business is implied (Broady 1956, p. 237).

Similarly they were apprehensive of a chairman as 'the one who bangs the hammer' but preferred to have an 'unofficial sort of chairman' so that they could 'all chip in'. Finally this refusal to ascribe formal status to neighbours is illustrated by the reluctance of anyone to check the balance sheet or inspect the cash books. The treasurer or organiser nevertheless insisted that they were checked to avoid 'insinuations'.

This example has been described at length partly because in itself it is a perceptive piece of sociological reporting and analysis, and partly because it illustrates so well the inadequacies of the middle-class accusation that the working class is apathetic with regard to organisations. It is clear that the working class can quite well organise instrumental activities; for example, shop stewards may well be the largest group of unpaid voluntary workers in the country, but they are reluctant when it comes to purely expressive activities. Apart from common problems and frustrations the residents of a town street have few interests in common. 'Nor in a modern industrial town are neighbours likely to have religious, political, cultural or other interests, sufficiently in common to weld them together as a social group, activated by a common purpose' (Broady, 1956, p. 238).

A number of studies have commented on the resentment felt if any one presumes to a higher status than that of their neighbours. In the Sheffield study there was a 'centrifugal pressure restoring the individual to the level of the group' (Mitchell, et al., 1954, p. 123). In Coventry aspirations to higher status may be deflated by reference to occupation 'Mr Dudley does think he's somebody, though. He thinks he's posh, and I don't know why, *because he's only a working man*' (Kuper 1953, p. 67).

In the traditional working-class community solidarity is the great value, greater even than leadership. Hence anything that is perceived as weakening that solidarity is disliked. Thus there may be a fear that involvement in secondary groups will weaken attachments to primary groups.

WORKING-CLASS ASSOCIATIONAL LIFE ON NEW ESTATES

Studies of new estates at Coventry (Kuper, 1953), Sheffield (Mitchell, et al., 1954), Oxford (Mogey, 1956), and London (Durant, in Pahl, 1968) provide some account of patterns of association among younger and perhaps less traditional working-class people. Men on

4

these estates are, as we saw in the last chapter, *status-dissenters*, who welcome the new opportunities, new demands, and a greater readiness to exercise choice, and who are willing to turn to impersonal agencies to satisfy their needs, to which they need have no feelings of obligation. These status-dissenters may be more ready to join formal associations, since they have lost the more acute class-consciousness of 'us' and 'them' typical of the more established and traditional communities.

Men on these new estates, who commute to different factories or employment centres, may not *feel* restrained by the social situation of their work in ordering their relationships with others when they return to the estate. Rather they will exercise whatever social skill they possess in choosing a pattern of relationships. If this is truly the case, then a fundamental change of attitude has taken place which would have direct relevance for the development of an associational life.

Certainly there is evidence from a number of sources that during the early days of an estate voluntary organisations flourish. Very often antagonism from without breeds association within. Common problems generate an internal, independent, social life. One of the early and best documented accounts of an interwar estate in north-west London describes the Residents' Association campaign for a 'Watling Garden City' (Durant, 1968). More specifically, such associations agitate for better roads or buses and play facilities for the children. In the Oxford estate of Barton there was a great deal of informal activity in the early days—baby-minding, lending, welcoming newly-arrived families, and so on: 'Out of this intense social activity, leaders began to emerge and to organise the children into cricket and football teams. From these men a Residents' Association was formed through the initiative of the Youth Officer of the City Council, and a movement began which led to the erection of a community-centre building.' The fact that it was the *men* who took such an active part suggests that the organisation was instrumental rather than expressive. (Mogey, 1956).

However, this vigorous local activity rarely lasts for long. In the discussion of the decline of formal associations in Watling a number of important points are made. First, although it was not difficult to get people involved in a campaign to secure amenities, it was more difficult for agreement to be reached on the administration of these amenities, especially since new residents had arrived who had not shared the failures and successes of the early struggle. Factional disputes developed and there was no institution recognised by everyone to which a final appeal could be addressed. Organisations catering for narrow family needs, or more narrow political and religious interests, grew up and competed with the Residents' Association. The economic crisis of the early 'thirties was an extreme form of the common economic problems in more recently-built estates, but it hit Watling hard.

In the early period, the major difficulties were common to all people. For many, however, adjustment to their environment meant to become acutely aware of their individual worries. The financial burden of a higher rent, more fares and instalment fees on furniture weighed heavily. The weariness of long train journeys made itself felt. Poverty loomed larger than loneliness. People were too worried to develop social interests, and often too tired to seek entertainment (Durant, 1968).

Furthermore, the rate of immigration slowed down so that problems of adjustment to the estate became an individual experience for each family and their solutions also were individualistic. To quote Ruth Durant again: 'People either completely shut themselves up in their homes or they went to one of the existing societies which competed for their favour. Each of these, whether it provided politics, garden seeds, or nursing services, was now a closed unit. Hence, by joining, the newly acquired member was helped rather than hindered in becoming "self-contained".' And not only were new arrivals moving in to this home-centred existence but also other families, who had perhaps played an important part in the early days, started to move away. Common objectives waned, together with the desire for collective action. An old resident summed it up: 'We have gone into our shells.'

Not only are residents' associations generally shortlived, but there is also difficulty on these estates in maintaining leadership in other formal organisations. Lacking experience of leadership, resentful of being 'pushed about' and yet reluctant still to stand out from the rest with the risk of being thought 'big-headed', inhabitants of new estates are not prepared to work towards the development of associational life. Even the affluent manual workers of Luton, studied by John Goldthorpe and his colleagues (1967) at Cambridge University, 57 per cent of whom own or are buying their homes, were not great joiners. Primarily centred on the home and the immediate family, they mostly participated in organisations of predominantly working-class membership, such as working-men's clubs, angling or allotment societies. The average number of organisations to which they belonged (not counting trade unions) was 1·5 for the men and 0·5 for their wives. There was hardly any participation in typically middle-class expressive or social activities.

INTERACTION BETWEEN MIDDLE AND WORKING CLASS IN FORMAL ASSOCIATIONS

Working-class primary groups, particularly kin, tend to absorb most of the energy available for sociability. Playing darts in a local pub or an evening at the Working Men's Club is more rewarding social activity than joining in voluntary associations. Having been a lower participant in the industrial world during the day, the factory worker is understandably reluctant to hear the confident tones of the manager's wife, fulfilling the call to community service of her girls' public school, urging him to support some worthy cause or engage in (to him) alien expressive activity. Inevitably such situations simply serve to remind manual workers of 'us/them' antagonisms. Those who do join middle class activities may be obliged, if they do not positively desire, to withdraw from the working class cultural milieu. Such people may lose the protective solidarity of their peer group culture without acquiring acceptance into middle-class culture. The working-class woman who agrees to play the part of a maid for the local dramatic society production, is not necessarily also invited to middle-class dinner parties and, even if she were, she might find it very hard to reciprocate.

The clash of norms which mixing in formal associations may involve is likely to create stress, which the working class may avoid through withdrawal or simply by not joining. The middle class are not only more articulate but enjoy expressing ideas in words and presenting a case convincingly. On the other hand, people from working-class backgrounds are less ready to accept that 'just talking will change anything' (the implications of this contrast may be seen as much in student committees and organisations as in various locality organisations). They will prefer to remain in their own class in their associational life in order to avoid being manipulated by the verbal skills of the others. Of course, middle-class people also expect to meet their own level in these associations: but it is also reassuring to them to have working-class followers, whom they can patronise and who remind them of their higher status in society. This confirmation of higher status is a reward middle-class joiners may expect to get from working-class joiners. We may expect the deferential working class to be more ready to join since they also may get a reward, if of a different kind.

Formal associational life presents further problems for the working class. Planning a programme of events over a period is a characteristically middle-class activity. They are more likely to see their life in terms of a career or series of stages and have learnt to plan their affairs as a normal part of living. They enjoy meeting the challenge of a problem and thinking of ways of overcoming it, whereas working-class people less readily view life as an orderly progression, simply because their jobs may hold out little opportunity for advancement and, indeed, the future may offer little security for them. Hence, it is not surprising that middle-class people take the initiative in making suggestions and running an association's affairs. If working-class people do find themselves as office-holders in such associations they are likely to rely very heavily on 'the proper' way of conducting business, accepting received procedures gratefully as a way of overcoming possible stress.

Nevertheless, the whole question of communication and contact between different class cultures is of great interest and is of particular concern to urban sociologists. The formal structuring of the work situation, determined by techniques, technology and the demands of organisational structure, puts severe limits on the type and pattern of social relationships—not only between the managers and the managed but also between intermediate levels in the hierarchy. It is in the non-work world of town, village or estate that patterns of formal and informal association may provide more direct clues to changing patterns of class behaviour. Do affluent manual workers, for example, join middle-class voluntary associations more readily? Do the patterns of urban segregation simply reinforce the distinction based on the work situation? What differences are there in a situation, such as a metropolitan commuter village, where physical proximity forces an unaccustomed awareness of different styles of life onto a broader section of the social structure, which would otherwise be socially distant. It is worth exploring this in some detail.

CLASS AND ASSOCIATIONS IN A COMMUTER VILLAGE

The organisational life of a commuter village is interesting because its small size and social heterogeneity bring groups with different social norms and different expectations and attitudes closer together. Proximity highlights the differences. In the central city or segregated suburb the middle class would not normally expect to have manual workers and their wives in their clubs and organisations. However, when members of the salariat choose to live in a village, part of their definition of the situation may include interaction with other status groups: indeed they may well consider the distinctive pattern of social relations to be the chief attraction of village life. Perhaps they expect deference as one of the rewards of upward social mobility. The working class, on the other hand, may be less inclined to play the role which is thus thrust upon them.

These were the kinds of questions I tried to document in a study I carried out in 1961 of the Hertfordshire commuter village which I called 'Dormersdell' (Pahl, 1965). The occupational structure in this particular village was very unbalanced, with a large group of professional and managerial salariat concentrated in an area of woodland about a mile from the centre of the village, where most of the working class lived on a council estate. Intermediate occupational groups were missing, owing to the high cost of privately built housing. Hence the terms 'middle class' and 'working class' could be used without ambiguity. The area of woodland was known simply as 'the Wood', this being synonymous with middle-class commuter. The geographical and social divisions were mutually reinforcing. The question of class differences did not have to be approached in a delicate or circuitous manner. The village schoolmaster said bluntly, 'We're a split society.' 'I expect you've heard of the difficulties between here and the village', said the wife of a technologist. 'The Wood people are energetic and run things and the village people complain; but they do nothing by themselves, so what is one to do?' Even the Women's Institute has two groups; one was described to me as 'in the daytime for commuter's widows—lots of cars and posh hats' and the other in the evening for the village. It was easy to understand how the takeover took place. As one village woman said, 'Nobody spoke to the villagers if they went and when there was a special lecture only people from the Wood were invited.' Because the Women's Institute has been taken over by the middle class, the Young Wives' Club of the Church is almost entirely composed of council-house tenants, thus confirming the division between the two worlds.

Not all middle-class respondents used the euphemisms of the Wood and the Village: 'It's a split between classes: the working class are more class conscious because of an inferiority complex . . . but anyway the old community has been killed by commuting.' The working-class people often make light of the two worlds, referring to the 'rich man and Lazarus', or, less clearly, 'Sodom and Gomorrah', in a detached sort of way. Some Wood people feel a responsibility towards the village and deplore the fact—as one woman put it—that 'there isn't quite as much linkage between the two sections as many of us would wish . . . it is difficult to get real cooperation from the village in many of the things that are done in this district'. However, others, perhaps too readily, accept the divisions in society. One man was warned before he moved in that 'You have to decide on which side you are batting—the Wood or the Village'.

A village woman, who is a domestic help in the Wood, saw things differently:

When I first came here I was the only stranger and it took over fifteen years before I was considered to belong. Now so many strangers move in and out every week there's no real feeling of belonging left. It's not just the Wood who change, but also the farm workers stay for only a few weeks or months. Perhaps that's why there's so much less independent life. We used to do our own entertainment until the Wood took over the Village Hall ten years ago. There used to be dances every week and now they're only occasional. The badminton is only for the Wood people. They tend to be snobbish when they've no reason to be: you know people when you work in their houses. There used to be fewer people here but you saw more of them. Now even in the pubs you must leave before the evening customers.

All this is rather enigmatic and sometimes overstated, but it does reflect views which were often encountered.

TABLE 6

Office holders in Dormersdell organisations (including committee members and church activities)

Chief earner	Number of clubs in which men and women hold office								Total households
	One		Two		Three+		No. inf. none		
	F	M	F	M	F	M	F	M	
Middle class									
London commuters	6	5	3	1	–	1	28	30	37
Local commuters	4	5	4	3	3	2	30	21	41
Non commuters	–	–	–	1	–	–	6	5	6
Working class									
Local commuters	4	–	–	1	–	–	24	27	28
Non commuters	–	–	–	–	–	–	6	6	6
Agricultural workers	1	–	–	–	1	–	10	12	12
No information									14
Total									144

Source: (Pahl) 1964.

It is important to understand more clearly how the people of the Wood see themselves. A thirty-year-old mechanical engineer, who had just moved in, summed up his first impressions as follows. 'It's a self-contained community: the wives form their own coffee groups, wine-making groups and so on. It's only 35 minutes by train from town yet it's quite secluded. We have the best of all worlds.' Another woman felt much the same: 'It's one of the most delightful places in the world. People of the same sort are all around, all very friendly: it's quite exceptional—people of the same education and income, who come out here for the same reason. It's near to London but a lot goes on here and it's well supported.'

Certainly Dormersdell is renowned for the wealth of activities which flourish there. Tables 6 and 7 show that both the joiners and organisers of most village activities are middle-class commuters' wives.

It is true, of course, that the middle class considerably outnumber

TABLE 7

Attendance at clubs and organisations in Dormersdell (two or more attendances in 12 months, church excluded)

Chief earner	Clubs attended by men and women								Total households
	One		Two		Three+		No. inf. none		
	F	M	F	M	F	M	F	M	
Middle class									
London commuters	7	8	7	2	4	3	19	24	37
Local commuters	10	8	7	3	9	3	15	27	41
Non commuters	–	–	1	2	–	–	5	4	6
Working class									
Local commuters	7	2	3	1	–	–	18	25	28
Non commuters	–	–	–	–	–	–	6	6	6
Agricultural workers	2	1	–	–	1	–	9	11	12
No information									14
Total									144

Source: Pahl (1964).

the working class, but it appears that in the working class it is only some of the wives of commuters who take any part in village activities. When considering office holders, the contrast between the classes is striking. As well as taking a large part in running the village, the middle-class men are also very likely to hold office in organisations meeting outside the village.

Although it first appeared that middle-class people are well integrated into village social organisations and indeed appear to run most of them, this is in fact a rather false picture of middle-class dominance, although one the working class seem happy to hold. Certainly this is the case in the Women's Institute, which has, as already described, been taken over by the middle class. The Badminton Club is also entirely run for and by the young middle-class men and women. However, this is no great loss to the working-class villagers: the younger ones monopolise the Youth Club and the Football Club and have good representation in the Cricket Club: the old age pensioners go to the Greenleaves Club (that is the women do, the men go to the pub) and a few older middle-class people in fact like to go and serve tea or act as treasurer without the indignity of becoming a member. Perhaps the only club where the village and the Wood meet on anything like equal terms is the Village Horticultural Society.

Sport is, of course, also a potential mediator between the classes, but there are few young people in their teens and twenties living in the Wood, since most of the immigrant newcomers arrive in their thirties. The church also provides some common meeting ground for the two worlds. Here the respectable, conservative working class is matched with a similar proportion of middle-class people. To summarise the interaction of the middle and working class in the social sphere, it would appear that by and large the working-class people are not *deprived* of any activity by the middle-class immigrants (if we accept the Young Wives' Club as a substitute for the Women's Institute), despite many activities taking place in which they are not represented. Because of this lack of contact each group accuses the other unfairly.

The wider, national class divisions in society are here played out in the local scene in Dormersdell. The contact between the classes becomes *less*, since however much the newcomers may try to be a middle-class squirearchy, the radical working class resent it, and the conservative working class find it no real substitute for the gentry.

The changeover from the hierarchical social structure, which was functionally suited to the village as a community, to the polarised two-class division may be the chief cause of the working-class people's resentment. The more traditional working-class element is resentful, partly because it has lost its clear position in the hierarchy and the reflected status of the gentry for whom it worked, and partly because it now finds itself lumped with what it would feel to be the less-respectable working class. This traditional group would like to be given respect and position in society, but get neither. The non-traditional working class see the segregated middle-class world as a symptom of the inequalities in society, and condemn all middle-class people as snobs and *nouveaux riches* without basing this on individual knowledge and experience.

The middle-class people come into rural areas in search of a meaningful community and by their presence help to destroy whatever community was there. Part of the basis of the local village community was the sharing of the deprivations due to the isolation of country life and the sharing of the limited world of the families within the village. The middle-class people try to get the 'cosiness' of village life, without suffering any of the deprivations, and while maintaining a whole range of contacts outside.

The middle class are inclined to view the local working class as props on the rustic stage, helping to define the village situation. Complaints about the failure of villagers to take part in voluntary associations have been alluded to. Such non-involvement on the part of the working class prevents the amount of mixing necessary for the middle-class definition of the village-in-the-mind and this is felt to be 'a pity'.

Many of the women have the sense of service to others, sometimes found in the squire's wife. On the other hand, to the working class they might just as well not be there. The main exception to this is the advantage which many working-class women gain in the way of un-taxed extra income from those middle-class housewives who employ them to clean their homes. This is probably the most direct form of social contact. Many middle-class wives claim to 'know' the village on the basis of their mid-morning talks with their domestic cleaners: the parallel with the white housewife in, say, South Africa, who claims to know about 'the natives' with a similar source of information is striking.

The middle class, despite displaying all the characteristics of class solidarity, vigorously deny class consciousness and point to all their efforts to join village organisations and play an active part in 'village life'. Thus national class divisions come into sharper focus in the local setting and this development by the manual workers of a consciousness of a common situation is what in chapter 2 we called the essence of the process of urbanisation.

CONCLUDING REMARKS

As always, it is necessary to introduce a cautionary note. The authors of a study of associational life in South Wales, found that class differences were not very important locally, or at any rate much less 'than experience of similar associations in England would lead one to expect. . . . We attribute the noticeably low importance of class to the provision by the chapels of a set of commonly accepted moral standards and conventions of social conduct, and to their functioning as what may be called "meeting grounds" for people of different social types who otherwise would be less likely to associate' (Brennan, Cooney and Pollins, 1954, p. 107). Similarly, Professor Williams did not find class to be a significant factor in his study of the Devon village of 'Ashworthy'. Sociologists may have been guilty of looking at middle-class organisations in a middle-class way, neglecting the importance of religion for the Welsh, the associations of immigrants and so on. The study in South Wales already mentioned, or the study of Sparkbrook in Birmingham by Professor Rex and Robert Moore add considerably to our knowledge of urban voluntary associations in specific milieux. Recent trends such as the development of middle-class pressure groups connected with state education or town and country planning are significant and need documenting.

Despite all this, the words of Simmel (with which we started) still need to be emphasised to those concerned with practical problems in localities: 'The lower a group is as a whole and the more, therefore, every member of it is accustomed to subordination, the less will the group allow one of its members to rule it.'

Priests, ministers, social workers, and teachers frequently use the word 'community'. As a notion it is generally held to be a 'good thing', particularly when it has a 'spirit' attached to it. Social leaders and public persons are usually very ready to pass judgments on the quantities of this spirit that they can detect. Local groups are congratulated when they have lots of it and preached at when they are said to lack it. In other words, the notion of community, or community spirit, is value-loaded: people who use the phrase have certain tacit assumptions, which as sociologists we need to make explicit.

In this chapter we will look at this notion of community from a number of angles. Does a community arise from the mere fact that people live near each other in clusters, and what does the concept itself mean? Does it arise from a common culture or from common deprivations? These are some of the issues which emerge from a discussion of the concept. Sociologists are by no means agreed among themselves on a common definition.

WHAT IS A COMMUNITY?

The street or the world?

If a community simply implies the houses and people sharing a given locality, then how are we to define its limits? Is an ocean liner or a holiday camp a community? If, on the other hand, the time element is as important as the space, how long do we have to specify? Some sociologists describe a community as a total system of social life bringing its members through the ordinary problems of a single year or a single life. Does this mean that our community is Britain? Would the Welsh, Scottish, and Irish agree? Are we not anxious to join the European Economic Community? And surely some of the most important decisions affecting our individual life chances are made by international bankers and financiers. What was the community in which we were living which decided to devalue sterling? Of course, most of the important decisions are decided by the trade unions, the Prices and Incomes Board, the Cabinet and such like, within a national system. But there is at present something of a popular reaction against such concentrations of power, with various pressures for home rule within a number of nation states: the Scots, Welsh, Slovaks, or Basques come to mind. In some respects the world is everyone's community; in other respects a more limited loyalty at a regional or national level appears the more meaningful.

Community as common culture?

Alternatively, we could consider community as an area within which there was a common culture and, more specifically, autonomous social control. Something of this type of community may be found described in Alwyn Rees's (1950) study of a small parish in Montgomeryshire based on fieldwork undertaken nearly thirty years ago: 'It may be said of many parts of the parish that every household is bound to every other by kinship ties, and these consist very often of more than one strand. To quote a local expression, they are woven together "like a pig's entrails".' Such a community of kinship and economic interdependence in a remote peasant-like community is hardly typical of modern industrial society. Ruth Glass has offered a definition of community as 'a territorial group of people with a common mode of living, striving for common objectives'. It is easy to see this in terms of economic interdependence, but, again, with our meat from the Argentine and tea from India, and with nationally negotiated wage rates, it is difficult to see a *local* 'community' having any significance. Yet even if the local 'community' has no economic or political autonomy, the sharing of common experiences may still bring people together with some sort of feeling of locality consciousness: the football team may help to foster more locality consciousness than anything connected with the division of labour.

However, where one industry dominates a place common experiences—strikes, lock-outs, unemployment, pit disasters—may serve to make people feel they share a common life in that locality. Similarly, tragic disasters such as floods or landslides (as at Aberfan) may also, paradoxically, engender solidarity and common memories.

Community as a defence against external threat

Conflict from without creates solidarity within. Where the national society in the form, for example, of a Water Board or the Ministry of Transport want drastically to alter the local situation, those who live there are more likely to unite to fight the common threat. People are then made to feel the community-in-their-minds and see a common purpose, associated with a closely defined geographical area. However, unless the local population has any power to achieve or boycott something, then the community-in-the-mind is simply a common delusion, shielding local people from the real world. Those with limited experience, who have not moved far from where they were born, may have limited social perspectives and goals and the more limited they are the more they may be said to be community-minded. Community, then, may be simply an ideology.

Cohesion through internal conflict

Conflict within a given locality will also serve to develop a common consciousness of living within the locality. The greater the intensity of conflict between different groups and categories within a locality, the greater will be their degree of involvement in that community.

The more people are highly involved in a locality the more likely it is that there will be intensely felt controversies, but also the more likely it will be that these controversies will be carried on within ordinary democratic processes. Personal attacks must be avoided where people want, or are obliged, to go on living in the locality. Ways of giving in without loss of face have to be devised and differences over issues must not be allowed to become personal antagonisms. Community identification helps to preserve the form of the controversy and also acts as a restraint or conservative influence on the outcome.

The greater the number of organisations and the higher the membership, the more involved people will become, since every association provides a pressure to take sides, thus not only drawing their members into controversy but also regulating the controversy and containing it. However, as we have seen in chapter 6, higher social strata are more likely to enjoy the verbal activity which joining such activities will involve. Controversy and locality commitment is thus likely to be related to class and life-cycle characteristics rather than being anything intrinsic to the locality itself.

Community of limited liability

'Community ties' may simply become 'negotiable commodities' for the middle class. Certain local activities may assume more importance for those who are most mobile, living in what have been described as 'communities of limited liability'. When there is a wide range of choice as to where people may live, it is more likely that people will assess the relative merits of places more carefully, particularly with regard to the availability of local facilities. These middle-class people for whom promotion at work or social mobility has been associated with geographical mobility gain experience of a variety of different localities. This wider experience may make them more critical of the local situation, more confident in taking part in locality activities and less afraid of offending those more committed, perhaps for life, to the locality. Also they can always move on, leaving their mistakes behind them.

Community as common deprivation

Unable to escape from the fact that in the community of common deprivation, for good or ill, a given collectivity will surround one for the rest of one's life, one is obliged to have a stake in the local situation. A whole series of delicate balancing mechanisms, cross-cutting ties, pressures and gossip serve to create cohesion out of conflict. The peace in the feud is the essence of this type of community. People cannot get out of it. This close-knit social situation may be stifling for some: and the social control which it involves is often welcomed by conservatives and deplored by radicals. In the nine-teenth century conservatives were afraid of the consequences of massing together large numbers of the working class, fearing lest their adherence to the central values of a capitalist society should falter. Similarly, in the twentieth century, radical intellectuals in socialist societies have resented being held in or sent to small communities where control of the Communist Party over their activities is so much easier.

The rich and privileged have always sought to escape from the community of common deprivation. Even if physically *in* small communities they are not socially *of* them. The so-called 'decay of the village community' was not thought of until the increasing wealth of the less-privileged enabled them to follow the example of the well-to-do. Darcy, in Jane Austen's *Pride and Prejudice*, offended his hosts when he remarked: 'In a country neighbourhood you move in a very confined and unvarying society.' However, Mr Bingley does not feel inhibited by this: 'When I am in the country . . . I never wish to leave it; and when I am in town it is pretty much the same. They each have their advantages, and I can be equally happy in either.' Later, Mrs Bennet, still smarting from Darcy's remark returns to the attack:

'Aye—that is because you have the right disposition. But that gentleman,' looking at Darcy, 'seemed to think the country was nothing at all.'

'Indeed, Mama, you are mistaken,' said Elizabeth, blushing for her mother. 'You quite mistook Mr Darcy. He only meant that there were not such a variety of people to be met with in the country as in town, which you must acknowledge to be true.'

'Certainly, my dear, nobody said there were; but as to not meeting with many people in this neighbourhood, I believe there are few neighbourhoods larger. I know we dine with four and twenty families.'

It is clear that the characters in Jane Austen's world lived in social *networks*, not communities. They moved about the country, staying in each other's houses, wintering in London or spending the season in Bath. The so-called 'rural communities' in which their friends' houses were located were rustic prisons only for those without the means to escape from them.

If, then, 'community' is simply a constraint on the less-privileged and that, with greater affluence and more 'choice', there has been a slow and steady move from community to social network as the meaningful arena for social relationships, what are the sociological implications of propinquity? This leads to a further type of 'community'.

Community as a locality-based social network

The importance of place, milieu, locality or what you will, in social relationships has concerned and vexed architects and planners in particular. And here again sociologists are not in agreement. If one poses the question 'How important is the small area where people live for patterns of social relationship?' other questions immediately arise. Thus we want to know how big an area is 'a small area'. Is it the town, the suburb, the neighbourhood, the block of streets, the street or the adjoining few houses? We also want to know whether we are concerned with the whole family and the places where they work or go to school, or whether we are concerned simply with those who spend most of their time in the area—the young married women with children under five, who do not go out to work, and those who have retired. Finally, we want to know what we mean by 'pattern of social relationships'—are these to be measured or assessed quantitatively or qualitatively? A daughter may visit her mother two or three times a year and correspond with her regularly. The same woman may also see local friends and neighbours nearly every day. How is one to assess the relative *importance* of these different relationships? Furthermore, even if some distinction is made between the 'real friend' four streets away and the somewhat annoying neighbour next door, is such information anything more than rather trivial gossip with very little sociological significance?

A well-known American study (Festinger, Schachter and Back, 1950) concluded 'the architect who builds a house or who designs a site plan, who decides where the roads will and will not go, and who decides which direction the houses will face and how close together they will be, also is, to a large extent, deciding the pattern of social life among the people who live in those houses'. This is what we mean by architectural determinism. The core of the fallacy can perhaps be best exposed by means of an example. Consider two identical local authority housing estates each with the same site-plan, access to facilities and so on. On one of these estates everyone is a status equal: they went to the same school together, they work in similar circumstances, they support the same football club and a complex interlocking kinship network adds a further dimension of shared experience. On the other estate, people have been rehoused from elsewhere; the generations may have been dispersed so that visits to parents and siblings take families away to a range of different localities; some men work locally, others travel a distance to work and so on. Loyalties and social networks extend over a wider area. The point that this example is aiming to make may be summarised briefly: the interaction community depends on the social system community.

Some preliminary conclusions

The discussion so far has been intentionally somewhat inconclusive and negative so it is time that certain themes were made explicit.

(*a*) The *meaningful* social area which people inhabit depends on class, life-cycle characteristics, length of residence, career pattern, type of social network and many other factors. That is, the locality social system depends, not surprisingly, on social characteristics. Thus the same physical situation will *appear* differently to different configurations of people with different social characteristics.

(*b*) Community consciousness may be engendered by certain social mechanisms stimulated by a threat from without, conflict within or common experiences and deprivations. Such mechanisms generate locality-based reference groups.

(*c*) Following (*b*), where a man's behaviour is related to the reactions of significant others, who live locally, and also interact with him in a number of different, yet significant roles, this overlapping of various social relationships provides the basis for locality social control.

(*d*) Mobile, middle-class people are able to escape from the community of common deprivation or social control. Such people inhabit a non-place community based on their loose-knit social networks, careers and consumption plans. Paradoxically, if community activity is measured by involvement in more formal voluntary associations the mobile middle-class may, in this sense, be highly locality conscious with specific demands and expectations.

THE OBJECTIVE BASES OF A LOCALITY SOCIAL SYSTEM

We have seen that the word 'community' serves more to confuse than illuminate the situation in Britain today. The economic interdependence of a feudal or peasant community does not exist; what we have instead is a degree of local social control and a community consciousness or local ideology, so that people behave as if there was an autonomy, which does not exist. Of course as the American sociologist W. I. Thomas memorably put it, 'Where men define situations as real they are real in their consequences'. Thus if the middle class *define* a 'village' as a situation in which one arranges and joins a number of clubs and organisations, then the situation may indeed differ in this respect from a suburb, where people, with similar social characteristics define the situation differently. One of the best descriptions of a community-in-the-mind is Arthur Vidich and Joseph Bensman's study of *Small Town in Mass Society* (1958), where the myths and ideologies by which people live are ruthlessly exposed.

Apart from such objective notions of 'community' the sociologist is mainly interested in the *objective* bases of a locality social system. This last phrase will now be used instead of the value-loaded word community. We may consider some of these objective criteria in turn.

The autonomy of the locality

What decisions on life-chances are made in the locality and who has the power to make them? This is a matter open to empirical investigation, but the two most likely areas where local autonomy can modify people's life chances are education, and housing and planning. Of course, it is true that each of these activities is related to its own encapsulated hierarchy of power extending up to the respective Ministers. However, there is sufficient local discretion over what proportion of central funds are requested for what projects, and in which order or priority, for there to be sound objective reasons for local conflict. Socialisation is a local activity and the facilities available for mothers and young children vary widely. And this variation, whether it be in nursery school places for children under five or awards to pursue courses in higher education, is not always directly related to the local rateable value.

Locality social status

Quite apart from national or international prestige rankings a *local* evaluation of status can still be of fundamental importance. Margaret Stacey (1960) provides an admirable account of a locality status system in her study of the changing social situation in Banbury, which we discussed in chapter 5:

Within the town the local traditional status system, under the leadership of the higher status groups in the middle class, rests upon a stable and a reasonably isolated society in which people expect to spend their lives (even if they were initially immigrants). They see their social goals in terms of this society and see them in relation to every aspect of their lives. Lineage, charitable work, local government service and public works generally, and club and pub associations are important as well as wealth and occupation. For it is a close-knit society in which family, business and social life are interwoven (pp. 162–3).

This provincial pattern is being undermined by the non-traditional middle-class immigrants for whom 'social status is not a matter of their total showing in the eyes of the town, but of their individual showing at work and socially in the eyes of their business associates, not all of whom are in Banbury and who for the most part are not involved in the town's close-knit social structure'. Despite this, Mrs Stacey felt that the traditional system had considerable strength. The advantages of being brought up to your position and of 'knowing where you are' are considerable. This provides the traditionalists in the upper and middle classes with a personal sense of security of position, which those non-traditionalists who have to maintain their position entirely on merit do not feel. The traditionalist wants to maintain his family position by segregating the socialisation and education of his children with an appropriate peer group. Yet non-traditionalists also accept this principle when they carefully select appropriate playmates for their children and send them to fee-paying or socially segregated state schools. They thus hope to turn their children into traditionalists by the second generation. This acceptance of the traditional principle of inherited class position will ensure, as Mrs Stacey puts it, that 'the traditional system and its values will continually and subtly change as it has done historically', but that it will be maintained. However mobile the middle class may be or become, the socialisation of children will remain a locality-centred activity reinforcing and perpetuating class distinctions.

Neighbours

Norman Dennis (1963) has questioned the need for neighbours amongst the 'new' working class of affluent manual workers whom, he argues, prefer 'to preserve the opacity of their domestic lives'. This reduction in a desire to interact with neighbours leads to a collapse of local informal social control: 'Neighbours are regarded as expendable in the search for middle-class success.' Now whether this is true or not is beside the point in the present context, since it is clear that the normal business of life creates emergencies and difficulties, which force some kind of relationship with those living in the immediate area. Even if the nearest kin or friend can be at an individual's house within half an hour, this may be too long if someone has had a severe accident or a fire has started in the living room. This may seem an obvious and rather ridiculous point to make but it is important to remember that, however much people are home-centred and live in social networks, some kind of cognisance of neighbours must be taken 'just in case'. Neighbours are not simply non-people like those that one stares through on an underground train. However, it does seem that the higher the social status the more this seems to be the case. Only those of similar social status are defined as neighbours. Those of lower status, who happen to live close by, as in a village, are simply ignored: they are not neighbours.

Facilities

Localities vary considerably in their range of facilities and people differ considerably in their ability to reach these facilities. Depending on the physical situation and socio-ecological system discussed in chapter 4, so people are differently placed with regard to shops, libraries, clinics, youth clubs, parks and so on. Even the distribution of branches of Marks and Spencers provides a pattern of unequal opportunity for a large section of the population. Access to these facilities is an important determinant of style of life and, given differential mobility potential and spatial restraints, so people's life chances will be affected. Many contemporary sociologists tend to underrate the importance of locality and implicitly or explicitly claim that class and life-cycle characteristics are sufficient to explain differences in ways of life. The whole of the argument presented in chapter 4 is relevant here and the socio-ecological system is one of the main differentiating factors between locality social systems. The distribution and availability of facilities is closely related to the issue of local autonomy, discussed in the section 'The street or the world' above.

CONTRASTS BETWEEN DISPERSED AND CONCENTRATED SETTLEMENTS

The settlement pattern has direct social consequences. Certain important social differences exist between areas of concentrated population ('urban') and dispersed population ('rural').

Availability of facilities

The poor in urban areas are deprived in a different way from the poor in rural areas. The lack of facilities and high cost of transport in areas of dispersed settlement are such that social welfare policies are likely to demand that there should be as few poor in rural areas as possible. Hence such areas are likely to become polarised between the poor, whose work keeps them there, and the richer people, who have chosen to be there (perhaps only at weekends and holidays).

Occupational choice

Where agriculture and related occupations are dominant young people may be inadequately socialised to adopt different work cultures or occupational styles. This may even apply to the relatively privileged sons of affluent farmers. This same point may, of course, also apply to other isolated occupational communities. However, whilst sharing some characteristics with 'solidaristic-collectivist' occupational categories, such as miners and dock-workers, the agricultural worker also shares much of the occupational ethos of those at the other extreme, such as lorry drivers and small shopkeepers, who stress individual autonomy. In areas of dispersed settlement and declining economic base, young people are obliged to leave for the greater opportunities of occupational choice and social mobility in urban areas. Even within the most rapidly developing parts of Britain there are pockets of economic stagnation, characterised by a flow of emigration and a gradual ageing of the population.

Social segregation and socialisation

Those in the most privileged positions in the occupational hierarchy are concerned to hand on this privilege to their children. Perhaps the most important means of doing this is to ensure that the early socialisation of their children is reinforced by a peer group of the same social status. It is considered particularly important, for example, that children from the more educated parents are able to practise the more complex and logical patterns of speech characteristic of their socialisation. Hence it is characteristic for the rich who live in rural areas to send their children to fee-paying private schools in order to reinforce their home patterns of socialisation. However, the professional or managerial middle class may find the cost of private education excessive and may seek instead the 'right kind' of state school, which has a sufficiently high proportion of children of similar social status for the same patterns of socialisation to be reinforced. Patterns of residential segregation help to ensure educational segregation; but this is less easy to ensure in areas of dispersed settlement. Thus those who want to use the state system of education may be deterred from moving into rural areas until their children have been through the educational system. The ease of reinforcing existing patterns of stratification will therefore vary between localities.

Some preliminary conclusions

A locality social system is related to the local distribution of power, status and facilities and there are important differences between systems. Class and life-cycle characteristics do not by themselves explain all differences in urban ways of life. This would only be the case if people with similar class and life-cycle characteristics had similar life chances in different localities. But this is not the case. Different local authorities have different policies with regard to education, housing and planning and private companies and public and private investors distribute their investment differentially between localities. The degree of mobility in and out of a locality has a fundamental impact on the degree of cohesion of the traditional status system. As people become more aware of these objective differences between places, particularly with regard to educational opportunity, so the backing of objective reality with subjective awareness will lead to common residence becoming increasingly associated with common interest.

On the other hand, localities where propinquity leads to no neighbourly relations whatsoever, where few or no kinship ties link people, where work and residence are separated and where political and economic power are also remote from the local area, then it is, indeed, less likely that a local social system will develop. But even in this extreme case, such as the area of single rented rooms in large cities, there will be an unequal distribution of facilities between such localities.

GENERAL CONCLUSIONS

Sociologists are concerned with social relationships. The actual pattern of an individual's social relationships may be described in terms of a social network, and clusters of social networks may, under certain circumstances, coincide with a territorially limited area. People associate with others to achieve common ends: where power over the allocation of certain scarce resources exists in a local arena, locality consciousness will develop. The development of the trades unions and the Labour Party during this century has led to a somewhat more equitable distribution of national power. However, the *local* control of scarce resources is still more likely to be in the hands of the middle class. Until the working class are involved in conflicts over such things as the local provision of schools or the local planning problems, so-called community consciousness will remain predominantly a middle-class ideology, shared by the deferential and traditional working class. The unequal distribution of power, wealth and prestige created by the occupational structure may be simply reinforced in a given locality—so that the less privileged are made even more 'less privileged' by differential access to facilities. Alternatively, the locality may have its own distinctive system of allocation of scarce resources based on criteria different from those which are most significant in the world of work, such as level of education training or skill. The ideologies of resource allocation in given localities will be considered in the next chapter. More research is needed on locality political and social status systems and their relationship with the national situation. The sociological significance of the linkages between the local and the national is a little-explored field.

Social engineering and the local environment   8

The neighbourhood as the immediate locality

In 1921, R. D. McKenzie, who later joined the Chicago school of urban sociologists, published in the *American Journal of Sociology* the first of five articles on 'The neighbourhood: a study of local life in Columbus, Ohio'. 'It is clear to me', he wrote, 'that the conception which the average city dweller holds of his own neighbourhood is that of a very small area within the immediate vicinity of his home, the limits of which seem to be determined by the extent of his personal observations and daily contacts.' McKenzie had asked his students to draw the boundaries of their 'neighbourhoods' and discovered the limitations of their mental maps. This work, which McKenzie did forty years ago, is still being replicated today, particularly by social geographers. Where people *think* they live depends on their age, sex, occupation, mobility potential, social network and so on. Not only does this conception change through time but also according to the stage of the family cycle: as social networks change so does the locality-in-the-mind. More recently, Peter Willmott (1962) studied the use of local facilities in Stevenage New Town and came to much the same conclusions as McKenzie: important social areas can be seen as a series of small overlapping local areas, which are different for different people.

Neighbourhood as a planning cell for the provision of facilities

Such conclusions are unexceptionable: the demands or needs of people for facilities follow definite patterns and these depend on the characteristics of the people concerned. The network linking up a particular family's home and the various facilities that its members need is part of that family's *activity pattern*. Certain thresholds for certain activities inevitably create a cell-like structure on the basis of which the provision of facilities and services can be conveniently distributed. Thus the London Borough of 'Chipping' may be divided into fifteen neighbourhoods, based on the distribution of primary schools, shopping centres and so on, and would have four 'super-neighbourhoods', with facilities such as covered swimming baths, which require a larger catchment area. The Chief Planner would structure the new Borough in this way to help him plan 'an even, equitable and convenient provision of services related to population'. He would be able to plan land use more easily, reduce the number of 'unnecessary journeys', and deploy local resources more economically, thus helping to make the Borough more functionally efficient. Finally, these smaller units would serve as a basis for local identification (see fig. 3).

If the idea of a neighbourhood or neighbourhood unit is limited to the convenient siting of institutions and amenities then it would simply be an important part of the planners' stock-in-trade and have no specific interest for the sociologist. It may be, of course, that people find the planners' unit too large to comprehend. In Willmott's (1962) study of Stevenage he found that, although 60 per cent of his sample used the local neighbourhood centres for weekday shopping, only 31 per cent, when asked what neighbourhood they lived in, could name it, although most of the rest could name their own housing estate (of which there are five or six to each neighbourhood unit). The functional unit does not, therefore, necessarily have any social significance in promoting 'community' or 'neighbourliness'.

Neighbourhood as ideology

There has been a consistently held misapprehension that somehow people would become 'neighbourly' if they lived in a 'neighbourhood'. Despite such notions having little to do with what sociologists have said or written, a number of authors have written as if sociologists *ought* to support them. Lewis Mumford is a social historian

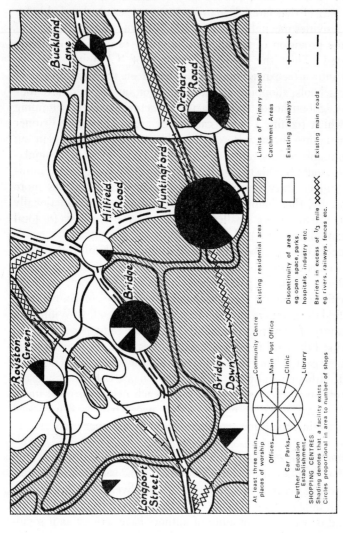

Fig. 3(a) Existing facilities in Part of the London Borough of 'Chipping'.
(NOTE: this example of the creation of urban neighbourhood units as the basis and rationale for the provision of facilities is directly related to an actual scheme in a London Borough. Since it is simply a planning proposal, it is highly schematic and the place names have been changed.)

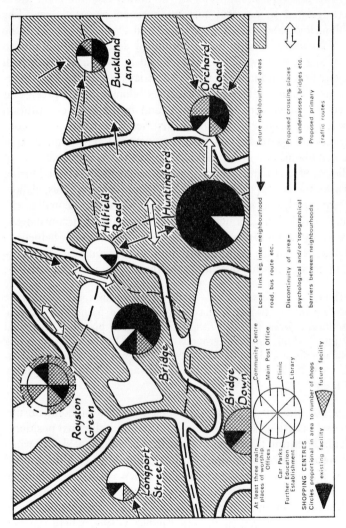

Fig. 3(b) Future Provision of Facilities According to the Planners' Conception of 'Neighbourhood', London Borough of 'Chipping'.

and social philosopher, who is particularly interested in urban planning, and is a typical supporter of the notion that the good life is directly related to physical surroundings. In an article on 'The neighbourhood and the neighbourhood unit', which appeared in the *Town Planning Review* in 1954, Mumford described the Radburn type of site layout, which was developed in the 1920s and which segregated the main movement of pedestrians and traffic in residential areas. People could walk to facilities 'along a spinal green that formed the inner core of the town, and by its very constitution furthered *face-to-face acquaintance*'. Notice that these social consequences are asserted rather than demonstrated. The population of these neighbourhood units was calculated in terms of the number of families needed at that time to support an elementary school. During the 1920s the New York Authorities favoured large schools, elaborately equipped, and so from 7,500 to 10,000 was accepted as the 'normal population' of a neighbourhood. Fortuitous circumstances, followed by architects' slavish adherence to fashion, helped to crystallise part of the conventional wisdom of planning. Mr Mumford, of course, has his own ideas for the size of a neighbourhood:

Five thousand *would seem to me* to be an upper limit. . . . Even if no further advantages to face to face association and friendly intercourse and *political cohesion* followed from neighbourhood planning, one could easily justify it on economic grounds alone. . . . In terms of educating the young and of making the institutions of democracy work the arguments are entirely in favour of a *mixed community* (Mumford, 1954, my italics).

It is not difficult to find many such examples of bold, unsubstantiated assertions by people in powerful and influential positions, particularly during the years following the Second World War when there were all sorts of hopeful idealists, aiming to create the good society, if not overnight, then within a very few years. The Chairman of Stevenage Development Corporation made a speech in 1947, which was quoted in the local paper: 'We want to revive that social structure which existed in the old English village, where the rich lived next door to the not so rich and everyone knew everybody . . .

the man who wants a bigger house will be able to have it, but he will not be able to have it apart from the smaller houses' (quoted in Orlans, 1952, p. 82). This coy refusal to use the word 'poor' and the paternalistic treatment of the deviant who wants a bigger house looks comic today, but urban sociologists had to struggle against these ideologies. Ruth Glass, who for so many years was the only British urban sociologist of distinction, made the point pertinently in her book on Middlesbrough published in 1948:

It is not clear . . . why the resuscitation of village life within urban communities should be regarded as being so delightful and so progressive nor how it is to be accomplished. . . . The mere shortening of the physical distance between different social groups can hardly bring them together unless, at the same time, the social distance between them is also reduced (Glass, 1948, pp. 18 and 190).

Thus, in the 1940s, non-sociologists asserted that physical proximity would reduce social distance, whereas sociologists argued that, if anything, physical proximity might even increase social distance. This latter point was documented in chapter 6, when discussing the social situation of 'Dormersdell'. Two studies in the early 1950s served to refute notions of architectural determinism. Leo Kuper (1953) in his significantly titled essay 'Blueprint for living together' showed that the siting of houses might provide opportunities for exacerbating antagonism just as much as providing opportunities for friendships. Similarly, the authors of the empirical studies on *Neighbourhood and Community* (Mitchell, *et al.*, 1954) concluded 'It does not seem possible to assert that the spatial position of the houses contributes one way or the other to the formation of friendships'. Finally, as Peter Mann (1965) put it in his sensible discussion of neighbourhood (p. 155): 'It is more useful to consider social relationships themselves rather than to worry about where neighbourhoods begin and end.'

A POLEMICAL EXCURSUS

Most recent evidence suggests that it is the small group of eight to twelve houses which forms the focus of positive relationships of either friendliness or hostility. There are also many indications that such clusters would benefit considerably if some extra communal space were available. If, for example, the development corporation or local authority left, say, half a plot-size vacant for each dozen houses they built, this space might be very effectively used. Following through the family cycle, it might first serve as the site for a shed, in which the young married couples might keep garden equipment and so on which they have combined to buy. Later it might be used as a place where the children's sand and water could be kept together with larger play objects. Small, carefully tended gardens would not then be covered in sand, and nor would the dirty feet of the neighbours' children constantly parade through the kitchen of the one child-centred household that does have sand and water in the back garden. Where living rooms are small and modern furniture is not designed for rough use by children, there is often a need for a larger meeting place, where a group of small children can play together in the winter or when it is wet. Formal play groups could even turn into mini- or multi-cellular nursery schools. Later the same site could be used as a place where an old car could be left as a plaything. Some sheds could be used by teenagers who wanted to strip their motorbikes and who need somewhere that is dry, can be locked and preferably has a work-bench and certain power tools. There could be more general workshops or simply places with a few chairs, an electric kettle and a record player. There is no need to expand on the possible uses of small pieces of wasteland or small sheds, scattered about the new developments. Any group of young mothers could add to the list—informal antenatal exercise groups, discussion groups and so on.

This idea of shed space for small clusters of houses is probably the only practical suggestion in this book. However, I have very little expectation that the suggestion will be taken up. Firstly, it will cost money and there is no guarantee that the plots will in fact be used. Secondly, it will look untidy—councillors would imagine, quite rightly, that a lot of messy shacks, piles of sand, old cars and teenage rowdy-holes might spoil the symmetry of a road of semidetached houses. However, these same councillors may well have large, spacious houses with plenty of room for the leisure activities of all the family; the garden may be big enough for their own children to have sandpits, a Wendy house in a tree or a work-bench in a double garage. All these things, which they take for granted for their own children, are certainly untidy but they have sufficient space, so that their lawns and flowerbeds need not be spoiled. Those without substantial properties have to make do with parks or recreation grounds, out of phase with the small-scale world in which, as the empirical studies suggest, most people live.

In other words certain values such as neatness, symmetry and order are thought to be 'better' for people. Large 'community centres' serving 10,000 people or more provide scope for an architect, make councillors feel munificent and can be easily incorporated into the itinerary of the police car on a Saturday evening. This is simply an example which students could perhaps discuss for themselves. The question which I am implicitly posing is 'For whom do the planners plan?'

SOCIAL VARIABLES AND THE LOCAL ENVIRONMENT

We have already discussed the main factors affecting urban ways of life in chapter 5. Figure 4 attempts to bring together the variables of age, sex, occupation, education, mobility potential and, in the case of old people, health. It will be seen that there are 170 cells, each a distinctive category, with different demands on the environment. However, this is simply an illustrative device and the number of cells may be extended enormously. Thus cells 30, 31 and 32 are categories of male adolescents between the ages of eleven and fifteen who are attending, say, secondary modern, comprehensive, grammar or public schools, but each of these categories should also be divided into social classes, determined by their fathers' occupations. Furthermore, demands for facilities, and hence activity patterns, will depend on the environmental situation. Thus, one might multiply the cells by, say, five different locality situations. It is not difficult to get 1,000 cells, each with distinctive and, to some extent, incompatible demands on the environment. Adding extra variables such as the

This diagram aims to suggest the bases for variation rather than to provide an exhaustive classification of social categories. Thus Parents' or Husbands' Occupation may be classified into five categories, which might be: 1 Professional/Managerial, 2 Intermediate non-manual, 3 Junior non-manual, 4 Skilled manual and 5 Other manual workers. Similarly, the Education categories 1-3 in block (2), Youth 16-19, might be: 1 left school at minimum age and no further education', 2 'full-time education to at least 18 but no higher education', 3 'university or other higher education'. The categories of Mobility might be: 1 full use of motor car, 2 shared use of motor car, 3 no car'. The two categories for Health in block (6) might be based on the ability to walk half a mile to shops or not. Blocks (1) and (2) are the offspring of those described in block (3). Hence, for example, the occupational structure should be proportionately the same in blocks (1) and (3) but not in block (2) where some young people are already at work. Ideally a multi-dimensional model would be required to express a more accurate representation of the interrelationships of the variables.

(1) Childhood

	Parents' Occupation					Education		
	1	2	3	4	5	1	2	3
0–4 yrs M. & F.	1	2	3	4	5	6	7	8
5–10 yrs M.	9	10	11	12	13	14	15	16
F.	17	18	19	20	21	22	23	24
11–15 yrs M.	25	26	27	28	29	30	31	32
F.	33	34	35	36	37	38	39	40

(2) Youth 16–19
(2A) 20–30 yrs unmarried or married without children

	Education			Job			Mobility		
	1	2	3	1	2	3	1	2	3
M.	41	42	43	44	45	46	47	48	49
F.	50	51	52	53	54	55	56	57	58
M.	59	60	61	62	63	64	65	66	67
F.	68	69	70	71	72	73	74	75	76

(3) Founding family (all children under 10 yrs)

	Husband's Occupation					Mobility		
	1	2	3	4	5	1	2	3
Wife	77	78	79	80	81	82	83	84
Husband	85	86	87	88	89	90	91	92

(4) Expanding family (children 11–19 yrs)

	Husband's Occupation					Mobility		
	1	2	3	4	5	1	2	3
Wife	93	94	95	96	97	98	99	100
Husband	101	102	103	104	105	106	107	108
Other	109	110	111	112	113	114	115	116

(5) Contracting family (no children at home, husband still working)

	Husband's Occupation					Mobility		
	1	2	3	4	5	1	2	3
Wife	117	118	119	120	121	122	123	124
Husband	125	126	127	128	129	130	131	132
Other (e.g. grandparents)	133	134	135	136	137	138	139	140

(6) Old age

	Health		Occupation of Husband Before retirement					Mobility		
	1	2	1	2	3	4	5	1	2	3
M.	141	142	143	144	145	146	147	148	149	150
F.	151	152	153	154	155	156	157	158	159	160
Living alone	161	162	163	164	165	166	167	168	169	170

Place

A third dimension to be considered at each stage.

A. Urban flats.
B. Urban high density.
C. Urban low density.
D. Small town.
E. 'Rural'.

Each with 170 Cells.

Fig. 4 Social Variables and the Local Environment.

length of journey to work of the chief earner or the type and number of dogs owned in each category would continue to make the cell structure more accurate and more complicated.

Therefore, when sociologists are asked by planners and others to tell them 'what people want', they are obliged to enquire 'which people?' People in different social categories will use the same facilities, potential for mobility, or whatever it may be, in different ways—and there is no evidence to suggest that these differences are getting less important. Indeed, there are signs that even when people of differing social levels get the same amount of money, they are often concerned to spend it in different ways simply to express their differences from each other. Thus, sociologists will tend to emphasise basic *constraints* and key variables, as we did in chapters 4 and 5, rather than attempt to do predictive market research for increasingly finely defined social categories.

'THE DEFINITION OF THE SITUATION' AND THE LOCAL ENVIRONMENT

There has been very little research by sociologists and social-psychologists on people's subjective awareness of a place and its importance to them. Professor Anselm Strauss has produced an interesting collection of *Images of the American City* (1961) selected largely from historical sources, and Dr. Terence Lee in this country has done some empirical research probing people's mental schemata of certain areas and relating these schemata to social class, age and length of residence (Lee, 1965). However, perhaps the most interesting study for present purposes was carried out by the American sociologist Gregory Stone who, as a result of a survey of women's shopping behaviour, distinguished four main types of consumer (Stone, 1954). These were:

1. Economic: a third of the sample were ideal-type, economic women. They simply wanted cheap, good-quality goods and efficient service.
2. Personalising: this type of consumer needed to be known in the

shops. She liked to be known by name and formed friendly and personal attachments with the sales people. She wanted to be treated in a personal and friendly manner. This group comprised 28 per cent of the sample.

3. Ethical: 18 per cent of the sample shopped where they felt they 'ought' to. They objected to the large chain store which was driving the little man out.

4. Apathetic: there was a remaining 17 per cent who just didn't like shopping and who didn't have sufficient interest in the matter to bother whether they were able to shop in a supermarket or a corner shop. (A final 4 per cent could not be put into any of the categories.)

These conclusions illustrate clearly that we cannot judge what people want until we have discovered their definition of an existing situation. We cannot assume that all people will travel to the cut-price stores or that the same consumer way of life will be considered equally desirable by all. In short, the social structure of society, by its very nature, gives rise to different styles of life and different definitions of the situation. The managing director and the man on the assembly line may each have a car and on a Sunday have the same mobility potential, but that does not mean that they will use it in the same way.

However, to return to Stone's study: he is mainly interested in the personalising and ethical consumers, and he seeks to isolate the variables associated with this form of locality-consciousness. (For example, one of his negative findings is that such people are not significantly differentiated by place of birth—it is not necessarily the village or small-town-bred woman who likes shopping locally.) He describes the *economic* consumers as young, socially mobile, lower-middle-class households with young children, who treat their present residence as something of a transit camp before moving on. The *personalising* consumer is likely to be a newcomer, to be older, and to have few or no children. She may seek friendly relations in the shops to compensate her for loss of friends elsewhere and is not expecting to leave her present home. The *ethical* consumer is likely to be of higher status and longer residence in the area. The deferential treatment from the shop assistants may be a reward such people are reluctant to forego. *Apathetic* consumers tend to be either downwardly mobile socially, or have been unsuccessfully upwardly mobile in attempts to leave the community.

Both the economic and personalising orientations to consumer behaviour are typical of newcomers to the area. The crucial intervening variables are aspiration, marginality and success. By this Stone means that those who see the local residential area as a short stopping place on their career up the social and economic ladder will be more strictly economic in their consumer behaviour. Newcomers, more marginal in their social situation, without high social and economic aspirations, will have a more personalised consumer orientation. These latter consumers did not have local friends and were not joiners of clubs and organisations, yet subjectively the place was very important to them.

From this example it is clear that the subjective importance of the immediate locality cannot be determined without careful research. Furthermore, the crucial variables associated with social mobility and marginal status, while being matters of fundamental concern to the sociologist, may not have seemed relevant to the planner. Indeed, this particular case of shopping behaviour may make him despair: planners want to be able to predict the demand for services and potential activity patterns of newcomers in new estates for which they have given planning permission. Ideally they would like a direct correlation between price of house and consumer behaviour. But clearly this is not a simple matter.

THE ENVIRONMENT AND MENTAL HEALTH

During the decade of the 1950s there was frequent reference in the popular literature to what was known as 'New Town Blues'. Put more precisely, the argument was that symptoms of minor psychiatric ill-health such as 'nerves', depression, undue irritability and sleeplessness would exist in a higher proportion of the population in New Towns and new estates than in older districts in the centre of cities. These assumptions prompted careful investigations into the incidence of neurosis in newly housed populations as compared with established populations. There was a remarkable congruity of results not only between studies but also between populations in the same study. In the study of a New Town and a London Borough conducted by Lord Taylor and Sydney Chave (1964) it was found that those who complained of loneliness and boredom in the New Town did so *because* of their poor mental health and not the other way round. Indeed, far from the immediate locality having an effect on newly-arrived immigrants, which later become less-marked as people develop social networks, Taylor and Chave maintain that it takes at least five years for any effects of the environment to become apparent. Furthermore, as with the population at large, it is women between forty-five and fifty-four who show the highest incidence of neurosis and not the marooned young housewife with children under five, as popular mythology maintains.

Taylor and Chave admit to being surprised that what they term 'the subclinical neurosis syndrome' had an equal incidence in a decaying London borough, in an out-country estate without local work or social life, and in a planned New Town. Thus they conclude that 'Social Planning appears to have no effect at all on the incidence of sub-clinical neurosis'. A later study by Hare and Shaw (1965) compared the mental health of people living on a new housing estate in Croydon with that of people living in an older central area of the same town and their conclusions were substantially the same.

Taylor and Chave (1964) maintain that neurosis is likely to increase if its incidence is expected and regarded as respectable, with plenty of kindly and sympathetic doctors to encourage patients and so on. Hence a New Town, with its favourable social provision, might be expected to provide an encouraging environment for the development of overt neurosis. The low figures are, therefore, even more remarkable.

Perhaps it would be appropriate to add a footnote to this section on the relationship between environment, housing and physical health. The Moser and Scott (1961) study of *British Towns* has demonstrated the differences between towns in the incidence of deaths according to various cause. However, it is essential to control for age, sex, and class composition of the areas being compared. It is likely that certain objective factors, such as atmospheric pollution, do have a direct relationship with the length of expectation of life at birth in particular areas. Particularly when low socio-economic status, overcrowding and atmospheric pollution all coincide, health conditions will be poor. Rural areas are still, in general, healthier than urban areas but the range is continuing to decline (Ferguson, *et al.*, 1964). However, modern authorities are extremely cautious in attributing a direct link between environment and health. As A. E. Martin (1967), a Senior Medical Officer in the Ministries of Health and Housing and Local Government, put it: 'Medical Science cannot therefore give very accurate comprehensive assessment of the influence of environment on health.'

PLANNERS' IDEOLOGIES

We have already seen from the preceding discussion that those with the power to affect the built environment have had distinctive ideologies. We discussed the ideology of community in chapter 7 and in this chapter we have seen it associated with the ideology of the neighbourhood unit. There are also the ideologies of neatness and tidiness, the ideology of good health and so on. The story of the early development of town planning legislation is well told in Ashworth's study (1954). And Ruth Glass (Pahl, 1968) has emphasised the peculiar anti-urbanism of the English, so that as a society we have not come to terms with the city but try instead to make it as much like the countryside as possible.

Planning the physical environment may be deductive, drawing up a blueprint for future development with the assumption that economic development leads to general social advance; or it may be inductive and attempt to coordinate public policies in several overlapping economic and social areas. Thirdly, planning may be utopian in orientation, aiming to create an existence of beautiful social harmony which, of course, has little in common with the real world, where resources are always scarce and hence conflict is inevitable. It is important to remember that very rarely do the facts speak for themselves. Facts reflect the values of their makers whether by the importance attached to them or by the sequence in which they are studied.

Planners always have values, whether explicit or implicit. The ultimate good is often simply taken for granted and it is rarely discussed or separated from technical matters. The government-sponsored study *The Expansion of Ipswich* (Shankland, Cox and Associates, 1966) is an example of explicitly stated values, since the planning consultants want to create 'social happiness'. They want natives and newcomers 'to get to know one another and to establish harmonious relationships for their mutual benefit' and they believe that 'social integration can be assisted by physical integration'. Readers of this book should be very sceptical of such statements.

The Strategy for the South East: ideologies and assumptions

In 1967 the South East Economic Planning Council published its first report for an area with a population of 17 million, a third of the population of Great Britain. We will take this as an example, in order to consider some of the goals and values which are taken for granted at a regional level.

The council is determined that the new and expanded towns which will be required to take a proportion of an increase of something like five million people by the end of the century should be thriving *social* communities. What this phrase means is difficult to determine although a 'cross section of the population' is good and an 'unbalanced' structure is bad. However, quite rightly, the council accepts the crucial importance of jobs. If firms cannot get the labour they require they will get 'discouraged' and won't move out of London. Hence the council argues as follows. First the 'right' social facilities must be provided—and apart from essential things such as shops and hospitals, 'community centres' are also considered to be the 'right' facilities. These facilities will then 'attract' the 'essential skilled workers' who must be promptly housed. Finally these well-housed and well-provided skilled workers will attract the firms. What happens to those in acute housing need in London, whether less-skilled or coloured, is not discussed in the *Strategy*. Planners in a mixed economy may be forgiven if they deal with problems one at a time. It will be seen that the basic assumptions are not questioned: it is simply assumed that certain facilities attract certain types of workers who attract certain employers.

Other ideologies, many of them conflicting with each other, may be found in the *Strategy* and this is typical of many other reports. Many of these ideologies are, of course, excellent, but the degree to which they conflict with each other is not always understood. First, responsibility is taken for social amelioration: London's housing problem is accepted as a collective responsibility. Secondly, the council 'see no place for a continuous or vaguely dispersed urban settlement'; they simply do not like it. Thirdly, there is an ideology of conservation or preservation which they take to be a 'real regional problem'. To some extent this is offset by, fourthly, the ideology of cost: they accept that there will be 'pressure to redevelop the site for very sound economic reasons'. Fifthly there is the ideology that the regional policies, which they propound, will serve as a solution to national problems. Finally, of course, there is the ideology of planning *per se*: the love of neatness and order which will produce 'a clear and recognisable distinction between town and country'.

Alternative professional ideologies

Foley (1960) has described three main ideologies in British planning. First, he argued that planners saw themselves as umpires or judges. They felt that they had to reconcile competing claims for the use of limited land so as to provide a consistent, orderly and balanced arrangement of land uses. Second, some planners saw their central function as promoting a more healthy and civilised life by improving the quality of the physical environment. Thus planners can happily retreat to technical and professional matters, such as the minimum space standards, which appear to them as activities of self-evident merit. However, it is not clear whether this improved physical environment is an end in itself or a means to some other social goal which is not specified. Thus, third, there is a goal, pursued by some, of providing a better physical basis for a better community life. Certain conceptions of what is best for people are held and these conceptions are primarily middle-class. Thus the 'best' community life is in small, reasonably low-density communities and so on; the concepts of 'amenity' or of preserving derelict medieval slum properties as part of a street-scape are also peculiarly middle-class values.

Planners are trained to be tidy and orderly and the notion of cultural pluralism and a diversity of life-styles and values, which is typical of modern societies, may be difficult for the profession to accept. Too often, bureaucratically-minded planners interpret their duties to the electorate as simply an exercise in persuading them that what they have done is right. Very rarely are alternative plans presented as a basis for choice. Professor Gunnar Myrdal (1953) has argued as follows:

Value premises should be introduced openly. They should be explicitly stated and not kept hidden as tacit assumptions. They should be used not only as premises for our policy conclusions but also to determine the direction of our positive research. . . .

They should be chosen, but not arbitrarily, for the choice must meet the criteria of relevance and significance to the actual society we are living in. Since as a matter of fact conflicting valuations are held in society, the value premises should ideally be given as a number of sets of coexisting valuations.

Sociologists could perhaps make their main contribution to social policy connected with the built environment, not by market research into activity patterns, but by the analysis of planners' goals and values and by the sociological analysis of the process of planning itself. Planners themselves are questioning the underlying assumptions of their profession (Reade, 1968). They are asking whether plans are simply bids for scarce resources, rather than alternative solutions geared to a realistic allocation of resources. The cost of implementing some of the large urban traffic plans is colossal: the figure of £250 million has been quoted for Liverpool, £200 million for Newcastle and £135 million for Leicester. It is doubtful whether we have the appropriate decision-making techniques for assessing the relative merits of different settlement forms and transportation systems, given the speed of technological innovation and change. No one would deny that there are critical problems and that decisions must be made concerning patterns of public and private spatial investment. The point which sociologists must not lose sight of is this: even the ideology of value-neutrality is an ideology just the same.

Planners cannot hide behind their techniques. They have different goals and different values: the technocrat or specialist also operates in a conflict situation with his colleagues. This is only to be expected when society itself is composed of conflicting groups engaged in a struggle over scarce resources.

Conclusions 9

What, then, are we able to conclude about the nature of British urban society? A man walking along a country path to one of the relatively isolated stations on a main line in the significantly described 'Home' Counties will be able to receive a certain pattern of stimulation from the environment. When he gets out of his train in the centre of London the impact on his physical and nervous system will be quite different. These obvious differences lead people to assume that there are fundamental differences between rural and urban society. It has been repeatedly stated throughout this book that sociologists are primarily interested in patterns of social relationships and the constraints and processes which help to explain them. What, then, are the fundamental features of British urban society and how are these expressed in terms of social relationships?

THE DISTINCTIVENESS OF BRITISH URBANISM

In the first chapter we considered urbanisation as acculturation, as some of the tribal British accepted part of the culture and way of life of their conquerors. An indigenous urban tradition emerged sometime between the eighth and twelfth centuries when distinctive social, political and economic rights were established in towns by custom and later by law. A distinctive urban tradition, specifically related to trade, developed in medieval England, which flourished in such centres as York, Bristol and London. However, two other major themes also appeared at this time. First, the landed elite continued to live on their manors or estates and did not necessarily have to live in towns or cities in order to consolidate their power. Second, the overwhelming importance of London led to the development of a distinct

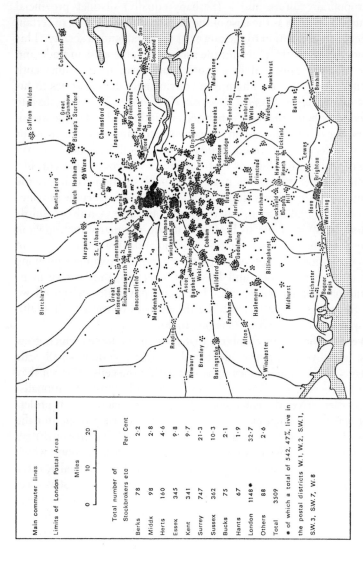

	Total number of Stockbrokers etc	Per Cent
Berks	78	2.2
Middx	98	2.8
Herts	160	4.6
Essex	345	9.8
Kent	341	9.7
Surrey	747	21.3
Sussex	362	10.3
Bucks	75	2.1
Hants	67	1.9
London	1148*	32.7
Others	88	2.6
Total	3509	

Main commuter lines ———
Limits of London Postal Area – – –

Miles 0 10 20

* of which a total of 542.47% live in the postal districts W.1, W.2, S.W.1, S.W.3, S.W.7, W.8

Fig. 5 Distribution of Places of Residence of Members of the Stock Exchange, Brokers and Jobbers.

metropolitan culture and a (perhaps equally) distinct provincial culture. The town as the base of the merchants' power was, in certain respects, in opposition to the power of the rural landed society. This tension between the elite and the aspiring middle class in trade and later industry appeared in a more acute form in the nineteenth century. As F. M. L. Thompson convincingly demonstrates in his book on the *English Landed Society in the Nineteenth Century*, despite the country being the most urbanised and industrialised in the world, the power of the landed elite remained dominant until the 1870s or 1880s. Indeed, some would argue that we are still basically an urban society with rural values, as we try to create villages in towns or, like the stockbroker pursue that most urban of occupations yet live in the country. Figure 5 shows clearly that, for those whose income provides considerable choice as to where they should live, a full two-thirds prefer the style of life to be found in the peculiarly metropolitan villages or small towns of South-East England. In a recent survey of the occupations of a sample of part-time farmers, owning land along a belt between London and Hastings, over two-thirds were managerial or professional people. The more physically urbanised we become, the greater appears to be the demand by those with wealth and power to own farms (Gasson, 1966).

We also showed in chapter 2 that even in the towns which grew most rapidly during the nineteenth century, certain small-scale 'village-like' characteristics remained within the cells of which they were composed. The British working class was basically traditionalist and conservative: the emergence of a class-conscious urban proletariat was more a matter of hope for the radicals than reality for the mass of the population. However, the *variety* and *diversity* of British urbanism should also be stressed. It is perhaps this latter point which is most difficult to convey in a book of this nature. Basically, these differences are related to the industrial and occupational structures of the towns concerned, but differences in tradition and historical experience are also important. How else could one account for the fact that Canterbury, with a population of 30,000 is a county borough, with the local autonomy that that implies?

THE LOCALITY AS A PATTERN OF CONSTRAINTS

In looking at modern urban Britain, we were more concerned to portray the constraints which the *urban* situation, as distinct from the work situation, imposed on the population. This pattern of constraints creates the urban social structure: the effect of cumulative constraints is to tie certain sections of the population to specific localities so that it is legitimate to describe a locality social system. The housing market imposes some of the most severe constraints on certain sections of the population: an incongruence between the housing market and the job market helps to create a distinctive socio-ecological system, which is the way the social structure interrelates with the spatial structure in a given locality. Different historical situations produced different locality social structures, which then become fossilised in the built environment. Hence people in the present locality are constrained by the social structure of the past.

In any given locality there will be a particular 'mix' of facilities, jobs, distribution of power, educational opportunity and so on. Men may be paid the same wages for the same jobs in different localities but their life chances will vary considerably. Some localities will have a wide range of alternative job opportunities and facilities; others will have limited opportunities, obliging school-leavers to migrate elsewhere.

The constraints of locality are less, the higher an individual is placed in the occupational hierarchy. However, the locality con-constraints increase until we reach those who are completely trapped in the so-called twilight zone of rented rooms in the centres of our large cities. Unable to change jobs because of their lack of training, their inability to get dwellings elsewhere and, perhaps, the colour of their skin, a pattern of cumulative and circular causation creates ghetto conditions unless there is vigorous intervention, with social policies aimed not so much at the physical environment but more specifically at ways of increasing social mobility. Geographical mobility is no substitute for social mobility: social policies aimed at achieving the former, without also being concerned with the latter, will simply transfer social problems to different milieux.

URBANISATION, URBANISM AND URBAN

Students may be forgiven if they are still somewhat confused by the use of these words and some attempt must be made to clarify them. For the last sixty years some four-fifths of the British population has lived in administratively defined urban areas. Thus urbanisation, defined as movement from areas of dispersed population to areas of concentrated population, or as a combined measure of migration flow and differential rates of natural increase, has long since ceased to be important. The study of the city is seen by some as the study of contemporary society (Glass, 1962; Reissman, 1964). Indeed, urbanisation, defined demographically in terms of population *concentration*, has now given way to urbanisation as a form of population *dispersal* in large-scale metropolitan regions. Stockbrokers in Surrey villages are *in* the country but not *of* it: coloured immigrants, living precariously in rented rooms, may be *of* the city but not *in* it, if they have no chance of social mobility within the urban system.

Urbanisation as a form of cultural diffusion is a particularly spongy concept: for example, it could mean the spread of middle-class values of personal autonomy and achievement or it could also mean the adoption of working-class values of us/them solidarity. Certainly there are trends in all modern societies, such as techno-logical innovation or the expansion of education, which are related to what some have called 'social change'. However, specifically *social* changes may be less dramatic: the man driving a motor bus may have a pattern of social relationships not so very different from his ancestor driving a stage coach. Thus I am arguing that the qualitative effects of quantitative changes are hard to assess and are not very helpfully described by terms such as 'urbanisation' which are almost impossible to define precisely.

Similarly urbanism, defined as distinctive social patterns, which are related to demographically defined aspects of urbanisation, is too all-embracing to serve any useful purpose. As we saw in chapter 5 the social processes which create urban ways of life relate to the whole society.

Finally, then, we come to 'urban': what do we mean by British *urban* society as distinct from British society in general? The answer to this question is provided by the book as a whole. We have stressed the way in which the spatial and social structures interrelate in an urban social system; we have considered a particular pattern of interlocking social and physical constraints which we called the socio-ecological system; and we considered the distinctive limitations on life chances provided by a locality social system. These issues are unlikely to be considered in other books in this series and taken together provide a point of view which is capable of considerable extension and refinement.

References and further reading

General

The following six titles are important for developing a better understanding of the main themes of this book.

BESHERS, JAMES (1962) *Urban Social Structure*, Free Press of Glencoe.

MANN, PETER H. (1965) *An Approach to Urban Sociology*, Routledge.

PAHL, R. E., ed. (1968) *Readings in Urban Sociology*, Pergamon Press.

REISSMAN, LEONARD (1964) *The Urban Process*, Free Press of Glencoe.

REX, J. A. and MOORE, R. (1967) *Race, Community and Conflict*, Oxford University Press.

WEBER, MAX (1960) *The City*, trans. and ed. by Don Martindale and Gertrude Neuwirth, Heinemann.

CHAPTER 1: *The Origin and growth of preindustrial urbanism in Britain*

BENTON, J.F., ed. (1968) *Town Origins : the evidence from Medieval England*, D.C. Heath; Harrap.

FISHER, F. J. (1948) 'The development of London as a centre of conspicuous consumption in the sixteenth and seventeenth centuries', *Trans. Royal Historical Society*, 4th ser. 30, 37–50.

LOWENSTEIN, S. F. (1965) 'Urban images of Roman authors', *Comparative Studies in Society and History*, 8, 110–23.

MILLER, EDWARD (1961) 'Medieval York', in P. M. Tillott, ed., *A History of Yorkshire : The City of York*, Oxford University Press.

PIRENNE, H. (1925) *Medieval Cities*, new edn. Doubleday Anchor Books, 1956.

SJOBERG, G. (1960) *The Preindustrial City*, The Free Press of Glencoe.

TACITUS (trans. 1948) *On Britain and Germany*, trans. H. Mattingley, Penguin Books.

THRUPP, SYLVIA L. (1948) *The Merchant Class of Medieval London*, University of Michigan Press; Ann Arbor paperbacks, 1962.

WEBER, M. (1921: trans. 1958) *The City*, Heinemann, 1958; first published in German 1921.

WRIGLEY, E. A. (1967) 'A simple model of London's importance in changing English Society and economy 1650–1750', *Past and Present*, 37 (July) 44–70.

CHAPTER 2: *The Emergence of industrial urbanism*

ASHWORTH, WILLIAM (1954) *The Genesis of Modern British Town Planning*, Routledge.

BRIGGS, ASA (1968) *Victorian Cities*, rev. edn. Penguin Books.

CHALMERS, R. (182–) *The Christian and Civic Economy of Large Towns*, 3 vols. London.

CHECKLAND, S. G. (1964) 'The British industrial city as history: the Glasgow case', Urban Studies 1, 34–54.

DAVIES, C. S. (1963) *North Country Bred*, Routledge.

DYOS, H. J., ed. (1968) *The Study of Urban History*, Edward Arnold.

ENGELS, F. (1845) *The Condition of the Working Class in England*.

FOSTER, J. (1968) 'Nineteenth-century towns—a class dimension', in Dyos, *op. cit.*

HAMMOND, J. L. and HAMMOND, B. (1917; 2nd edn. 1925) *The Town Labourer 1760–1832*, Longmans; reprint edn. 1966.

GLASS, R. (1968) 'Urban Sociology in Great Britain', in R. E. Pahl, ed., *Readings in Sociology*, Pergamon Press.

LASLETT, PETER (1965) *The World We Have Lost*, Methuen.

MARSHALL, J. D. (1968) 'Colonisation as a factor in the planting of towns in North-West England', in Dyos, *op. cit.*

ROSSER, C. and HARRIS, C. (1965) *The Family and Social Change: a study of family and kinship in a South Wales town*, Routledge.

WEBER, A. F. (1899) *The Growth of Cities in the Nineteenth Century*; reprint edn., Cornell Paperbacks (O.U.P.).

Some contemporary studies of urbanisation

BREESE, G., ed. (1969) *The City in Newly Developing Countries*, Prentice-Hall.

EPSTEIN, A. L. (1958) *Politics in an Urban African Community*, Manchester University Press.

HAUSER, P. M., ed. (1961) *Urbanization in Latin America*, Unesco.

HAUSER, P. M. and SCHNORE, L. F., eds. (1965) *The Study of Urbanization*, Wiley.

LITTLE, K. L. (1965) *West African Urbanization*, Cambridge University Press.

SOUTHALL, A., ed. (1961) *Social Change in Modern Africa*, Oxford University Press.

CHAPTER 3: *The sociographic pattern*

BURGESS, E. W. (1925) 'The growth of the city' in Park, R. E. (1925) *op. cit.*

COLLISON, P. (1960) 'Occupation, education and housing in an English city', *American Journal of Sociology*, 65, 588–97.

COLLISON, P. and MOGEY, J. (1959) 'Residence and social class in Oxford', *American Journal of Sociology*, 64, 599–605.

DICKINSON, R. E. (1964) *City and Region*, Routledge.

GEORGE, M. DOROTHY (1965) *London Life in the Eighteenth Century*, Penguin. First published Kegan Paul, Trench, Trubner, 1925.

GITTUS, E. (1965) 'An experiment in the identification of urban sub-areas', *Trans. of the Bartlett Society*, 2, 107–35.

HERAUD, B. J. (1968) 'Social class and the new towns', *Urban Studies*, 5, 33–53.

JONES, E. (1960) *A Social Geography of Belfast*, Oxford University Press.

JONES, E. (1966) *Towns and Cities*, Oxford University Press.

MORRIS, T. (1958) *The Criminal Area : a study in social ecology*, Routledge.

PARK, R. E. (1952) *Human Communities*, Free Press of Glencoe.

PARK, R. E., *et al.* (1925) *The City*, University of Chicago Press; reprinted 1967.

THEODORSON, G. A., ed. (1961) *Studies in Human Ecology*, Row, Peterson.

WESTERGAARD, J. H. (1964) 'The structure of Greater London', in *London : aspects of change*, ed. by the Centre for Urban Studies, MacGibbon & Kee.

Note. The Centre for Urban Studies is currently engaged in the third Survey of London Life and Labour. The first volume, on *The Socio-Geographical Pattern*, edited by Mrs Ruth Glass, will supersede the article by Westergaard. The *Atlas of London and the London Region* prepared under the direction of Emrys Jones and D. J. Sinclair (Pergamon 1969) provides an unrivalled picture of the sociogeographic pattern of a great metropolis.

CHAPTER 4: *Housing classes and the socio-ecological system*

BESHERS, J. M. (1962) *Urban Social Structure*, Free Press of Glencoe.

CHAPMAN, D. (1955) *The Home and Social Status*, Routledge.

CHOMBART DE LAUWE, P., *et al.* (1960) *Famille et habitation, vol. 2, Un Essai d'observation experimentale*, Paris, Centre National de la Recherche Scientifique.

CHORLEY, K. (1950) *Manchester Made Them*, Faber and Faber.

DONNISON, D. V. (1967) *The Government of Housing*, Penguin Books.

KUPER, L. (1953) 'Blueprint for living together', in L. Kuper, ed., *Living in Towns*, Cresset Press.

MILNER HOLLAND REPORT (1965) *Housing in Greater London*, Cmnd. 2605, H.M.S.O.

MUSIL, J. (1968) 'The development of Prague's ecological structure', in Pahl, ed., *op. cit.*

PAHL, R. E. (1966) 'The social objectives of village planning', *Official Architecture and Planning*, 29, 1146–50.

PAHL, R. E., ed. (1968) *Readings in Urban Sociology*, Pergamon Press.

REX, J. A. 'The sociology of a zone in transition', in Pahl, ed., *op. cit.*

REX, J. A. and MOORE, R. (1967) *Race, Community and Conflict*, Oxford University Press.

GOLDTHORPE, J. H. (1966) 'Attitudes and behaviour of car assembly workers: a deviant case and a theoretical critique', *British Journal of Sociology*, 17, 227–44.

HOGGART, R. (1958) *The Uses of Literacy*, Penguin Books edition.

CHAPTER 5: *Urban ways of life in Britain*

ABRAMS, M. (1964) 'Changing needs of different age groups', in *Communities and Social Change*, National Council of Social Service.

BOTT, E. (1957) *Family and Social Network*, Tavistock.

FRANKENBERG, F. (1966) *Communities in Britain*, Penguin Books.

GOLDTHORPE, J. H., LOCKWOOD, D., BECHHOFER, F., and PLATT, J. (1968) *The Affluent Worker*, Cambridge University Press.

KLEIN, J. (1965) *Samples from English Culture*, Routledge.

LITTLEJOHN, J. (1964) *Westrigg: the sociology of a Cheviot parish*, Routledge.

MOSER, C. A. and SCOTT, W. (1961) *British Towns*, Oliver & Boyd.

NEWSON, J. and NEWSON, E. (1963) *Infant Care in an Urban Community*, Allen & Unwin; Penguin Books 1965.

ROSSER, C., and HARRIS, C. (1965) *The Family and Social Change*, Routledge.

RUNCIMAN, W. G. (1966) *Relative Deprivation and Social Justice*, Routledge.

STACEY, M. (1960) *Tradition and Change*, Oxford University Press.

VEREKER, C., MAYS, J. B., GITTUS, E., and BROADY, M., (1961), *Urban Redevelopment* etc., Liverpool University Press.

WILENSKY, H. L. (1960) 'Work, careers and social integration', *International Social Science Journal*, 42, 543–60.

WILENSKY, H. L. (1961) 'Orderly careers and social participation: the impact of work history on social integration in the middle mass', *American Sociological Review*, 26, 521–39.

YOUNG, M. and WILLMOTT, P. (1962) *Family and Kinship in East London*, Penguin Books Edition.

CHAPTER 6: *Formal voluntary associations*

BIRCH, A. H. (1959) *Small Town Politics*, Oxford University Press.

BOTTOMORE, T. (1954) 'Social Stratification in voluntary organizations', in D. V. Glass, ed., *Social Mobility in Britain*, Routledge.

BRENNAN, T., COONEY, E. W. and POLLINS, H. (1954) *Social Change in South-West Wales*, Watts.

BROADY, M. (1956) 'The organisation of Coronation street parties', *Sociological Review* 4, 223–42.

CAUTER, T. and DOWNHAM, J. S. (1954) *The Communication of Ideas*, Chatto & Windus.

DENNIS, N. (1961) 'Changes in function and leadership renewal', *Sociological Review*, 9, 55–84.

DURANT, R. (1968) 'Community and association in a London housing estate', in R. E. Pahl, ed., *Readings in Urban Sociology*, Pergamon Press.

GOLDTHORPE, J. H., *et al.* (1967) 'The affluent worker and the thesis of *embourgeoisement*: some preliminary research findings', *Sociology*, 1, 11–31.

KLEIN, J. (1965) *Samples from English Cultures*, vol. I. Routledge.

KUPER, L. (1953) 'Blueprint for living together', in L. Kuper, ed., *Living in Towns*, Cresset Press.

MITCHELL, G. D., LUPTON, T., HODGES, M. W. and SMITH, C. S. (1954) *Neighbourhood and Community. An enquiry into social relationships on housing estates in Liverpool and Sheffield*, Liverpool University Press.

MOGEY, J. M. (1956) *Family and Neighbourhood: two studies in Oxford*, Oxford University Press.

PAHL, R. E. (1964) 'The two class village', *New Society*, 27 Feb.

PAHL, R. E. (1965) 'Class and community in English commuter villages', *Sociologia Ruralis*, 5, 5–23.

REX, J. and MOORE, R. (1967) *Race, Community and Conflict*, Oxford University Press, chapter 7.

SIMMEL, G. (trans. 1950) *The Sociology of George Simmel*, ed. and trans. K. Wolff, Free Press of Glencoe.

STACEY, M. (1960) *Tradition and Change*, Oxford University Press, chapter 5.

WILLMOTT, P., and YOUNG, M. (1960) *Family and Class in a London Suburb*, Routledge.

CHAPTER 7: *Community and locality*

Discussions of 'community'

DENNIS, N. (1968) 'The popularity of the neighbourhood community idea', in R. E. Pahl, ed., *Readings in Urban Sociology*, Pergamon Press.
MORRIS, R. N. and MOGEY, J. (1965) *The Sociology of Housing*, Routledge.

Studies of communities of common deprivation and social control

FRANKENBERG, R. (1957) *Village on the Border*, Cohen & West.
REES, A. (1950) *Life in a Welsh Countryside*, University of Wales Press.

Studies of locality social systems

ELIAS, N. and SCOTSON, J. L. (1965) *The Established and the Outsiders*, Frank Cass.

STACEY, MARGARET (1960) *Tradition and Change: a study of Banbury*, Oxford University Press.

WILLIAMS, W. M. (1956) *The Sociology of an English Village: Gosforth*, Routledge.

Interesting discussion of the American literature

WARREN, R. L. (1963) *The Community in America*, Rand McNally.

Additional references

DENNIS, N. (1963) 'Who needs neighbours?' *New Society*, 43, July.

FESTINGER, L., SCHACHTER, S. and BACK, K. (1950) *Social Pressures in Informal Groups*, Harper, N.Y.

VIDICH, A. and BENSMAN, J. (1958) *Small Town in Mass Society*, Princeton University Press; Doubleday Anchor Books, 1960.

WILLIAMS, W. M. (1963) *A West Country Village: Ashworthy*, Routledge.

CHAPTER 8: *Social Engineering and the local environment*

ASHWORTH, W. (1954) *The Genesis of Modern British Town Planning*, Routledge.

FERGUSON, T., *et al.* (1964) *Public Health and Urban Growth*, The Centre for Urban Studies.

FOLEY, D. L. (1960) 'British town planning: one ideology or three?' *British Journal of Sociology*, 11, 211–31.

GLASS, R. (1968) 'Urban sociology in Great Britain', rev. and reprinted in R. E. Pahl, ed., *Readings in Urban Sociology*, Pergamon Press.

GLASS, R., ed. (1948) *The Social Background of a Plan*, Routledge.

HARE, E. H. and SHAW, G. K. (1965) *Mental Health on a New Housing Estate*, Oxford University Press.

LEE, T. R. (1965) 'Psychology and Living space', *Trans. of the Bartlett Society*, 2, 9–36.

MCKENZIE, R. D. (1921–22) 'The neighbourhood: a study of local life in Columbus, Ohio', *American Journal of Sociology*, 27, 145–63, 344–63, 486–509, 588–609, 780–99.

MANN, P. H. (1965) *An Approach to Urban Sociology*, Routledge, esp. chapter 6, 'Focus on the neighbourhood'.

MARTIN, A. E. (1967) 'Environment, housing and health', *Urban Studies*, 4, 1–21.

MITCHELL, G. D., LUPTON, T., HODGES, M. W. and SMITH, C. S. (1954) *Neighbourhood and Community. An enquiry into social relationships on housing estates in Liverpool and Sheffield*, Liverpool University Press.

MORRIS, R. N. and MOGEY, J. (1965) *The Sociology of Housing*, Routledge.

MUMFORD, L. (1954) 'The neighbourhood and the neighbourhood unit', *Town Planning Review*, 24, 256–69.

MYRDAL, GUNNAR (1953) *British Journal of Sociology*, 210–242.

MOSER, C. A. and SCOTT, W. (1961) *British Towns*, Oliver & Boyd.

ORLANS, H. (1952) *Stevenage: a sociological study of a new town*, Routledge.

READE, ERIC (1968) 'Some notes toward a sociology of planning—the case for self-awareness', *Journal of the Town Planning Institute*, 54, 214–18.

SOUTH EAST PLANNING COUNCIL (1967) *The Strategy for the South East*, H.M.S.O.

STONE, G. P. (1954) 'City shoppers and urban identification: observations on the social psychology of city life', *American Journal of Sociology*, 60, 36–45.

STRAUSS, A. (1961) *Images of the American City*, Free Press of Glencoe.

TAYLOR, Lord, and CHAVE, S. (1964) *Mental Health and Environment*, Longmans.

WILLMOTT, P. (1962) 'Housing density and town design in a new town' *Town Planning Review*, 33, 115–27.

CHAPTER 9: *Conclusions*

GASSON, RUTH (1966) *The Influence of Urbanization on Farm Ownership and Practice*, Department of Agricultural Economics, Wye College (University of London), *Studies in Rural Land Use* Report No. 7.

GLASS, R. (1962) 'Urban sociology', in A. T. Welford, *et al.*, eds., *Society*, Routledge.

THOMPSON, F. M. L. (1963) *English Landed Society in the Nineteenth Century*, Routledge.

Index